CUTWATER

SPEEDBOATS AND LAUNCHES FROM THE GOLDEN AGE OF BOATING

Text and Photography by Robert Bruce Duncan

First published in 1993 by
Top Ten Publishing Corporation,
42 Digital Drive, Suite 5,
Novato, California 94949, USA

THE
TOP
TEN

© *Robert Bruce Duncan, 1993*

Printed in Hong Kong

The information contained in
this publication is correct to the
best of our knowledge. Both
author and publisher, however,
disclaim any liability incurred as
a result of its use. The publisher
acknowledges that certain words
and model designations are
the property of the trademark
holder. This book is not an
official publication.
ISBN 1-879301-04-0
Library of Congress Catalog Card Number: 92-84099

P R E F A C E

The Magic Of Old Wooden Boats

These are the boats of the long golden summers, of mirror glassy waters, of island summer houses with cool verandas. Boats of immodest beauty from days of innocence. Wood and steel, leather and bronze. Honest in simplicity and understatement, loud and powerful and fast, designed and built with one intent: to make people happy.

Icons, perhaps, but not in the sense that they are meant to be worshiped. Icons because they've been conceived with love; built with craftsmanship, care, and attention to detail; used with great joy; restored with equal love; and flattered and pampered and esteemed for 50 or 60 or 80 years. Icons because they are more than just old boats, more even than vibrant links to the past.

To the ancients, it was obvious that any object of attention and love had the ability to reflect the love it had received, bestowing happiness on those around it. Something like this may explain the magic of old wooden boats.

Or perhaps it's the *anima*, the female spirit within the boat, that bestows such pleasure. Strong and unabashed and powerful, like *Baby Bootlegger* or *Miss Columbia*, but feminine nonetheless: revelling in use, responsive, cranky sometimes, curvaceous in design, needing almost daily attention, and seductive beyond words.

But one suspects there's a simpler explanation for the magic of these beauties: antique wooden boats are just plain fun. Fun to look at, fun to touch, fun to show off with, fun to talk about. Fun on perfect days, fun when a breeze whips a chop on the water and you gun the engine and dance across the top of the swell.

Sunny, summer, spray-in-your-face fun.

C O N T E N T S

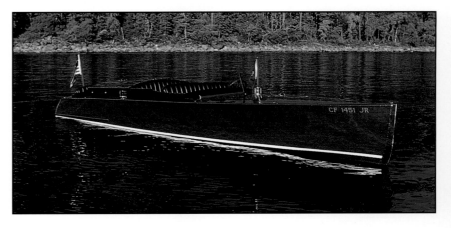

DEAD MEN &
LIVING BOATS

As much as this is a book about boats, it is also a book about people. While the boats are still here, both in the physical sense, running the lakes and rivers, and in the photographic sense, pictured in this book, most of the men are gone. This book is testimony to the legacy of these men.

Men who designed with God-given inspiration, built with loving hands, and raced with reckless abandon.

Men whose obsession with beauty, craftsmanship, and the persistent competition between water and speed many times outran the pace of practical realism.

Certainly there were those among them governed by the iron rule of practicality. Men whose firm grasp of the bottom line ensured survival through the economic panic of 1921-22, and through the Great Depression. But, as often as not, the pioneers of power boating were artists, men governed by their passions.

This is a story of human creativity and the external limitations within which creativity flourishes. By its very nature the story of both success and heartbreak. The story of brief bursts of productivity alternating with periods of frustration. A story of the fickle gift of the creative muse.

John L. Hacker, thought by many the most gifted of American speedboat builders, designed boats for innumerable incarnations and reincarnations of the Hacker Boat Company. And for Greavette, for Dodge, for almost anyone who appreciated the subtle and discrete lines that remain the hallmark of any Hacker designed boat.

Considered by many the epitome of early racing design, Hacker's three-time Gold Cup winner *El Lagarto* now makes her home in the Adirondack Museum, lost perhaps forever from the world of water and speed, but on a daily basis enriching the lives of museumgoers. And she's only one of Hacker's quiet masterpieces. This is a story of persistence.

Hubert Charles "Bert" Minett, of Bracebridge, Muskoka, Ontario, was a notoriously impractical builder; it is said that a boat left his shop only after he was satisfied that it was as perfect as it could possibly be. There is no

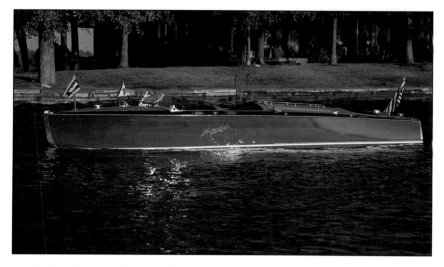

doubt that his propitious 1925 partnership with Bryson Shields, a businessman with a keen eye for profit margins, extended Minett's boatbuilding longevity. This is the story of a symbiotic relationship, the artist in partnership with the practical man.

With the benefit of royalties from his invention of the hydraulic dump-truck lift, Gar Wood survived the depression to race until 1935 when he announced his retirement. His name became synonymous with victory in powerboat racing. and his almost inevitable victory in the Gold Cup precipitated a 1921 rule change intended to eliminate his competitiveness.

Doubtless though, his dedication to speed overstepped the bounds of the rational. In 1928, 17 days before the Harmsworth Trophy meet, Gar Wood and Orlin Johnson, his riding mechanic — the legendary "wrench" — crashed in *Miss America VI*. More logical men would have questioned the sanity of even stepping aboard this 2,200 horsepower, twin Packard aircraft engine-powered, fire-breathing behemoth. Both men were injured, Johnson seriously. On race day, little more than two-and-a-half weeks later, Johnson,

his broken jaw still in a cast, ribs taped, and head bandaged, was lifted into a new boat — with the same Packards — to co-pilot and win the Harmsworth Trophy.

Perhaps it is easier to understand the commitment of the man at the helm. Many are willing to challenge death when at the wheel. Few are willing to go along for the ride. This is the story of Gar Wood's obsession and innovation rewarded. And the story of Orlin Johnson's faith.

Christopher Columbus "Chris" Smith, the patriarch whose family gave birth to Chris-Craft, seemed little concerned with financial success. Once Chris-Craft had brought the enjoyment of boating to the little man, to the middle-class family, Smith was happy to hang out in the boiler room of his factory, informally dressed, enjoying the pleasure of his odiferous cigars.

But Smith had always been a man of intuition, non-technical in his approach. While he is sometimes — and wrongly — credited with building in 1910 what is thought to be the first American single-step hydroplane,

Reliance III (a derivative of William Henry Fauber's innovative 1908 seven-step hull design), he openly admitted that he knew little and cared less for complicated theories of friction, wetted surface, and displacement.

Smith designed by trial and error and built for quality — two proven techniques. His choice of partners was less orthodox. Speed-obsessed, diamond-studded and definitely flashy, Johnny J. "Baldy" Ryan was Chris Smith's first patron. As partners Smith and Ryan led the way in early American powerboat racing. Their *Reliance* boats proved that bigger was not necessarily faster. It was perhaps poetic justice that the gods called in the chips on "Baldy" Ryan; his fortune dissipated, he disappeared from the history of power boating. But the legacy of Baldy and Chris remains — the entrepreneur and the intuitive craftsman.

Certainly there were, however, men who listened both to the muse and to the voice of worldly wisdom. George Crouch, designer of *Baby Bootlegger*, *Teaser*, and *Miss Columbia*, remained an academician teaching

mathematics at the Webb Institute and Columbia University. Restored by Mark Mason, Crouch's *Baby Bootlegger* is the most desirable antique powerboat in the nation. *Teaser*, now owned by Hal Orchard, an ACBS judge, can sometimes be seen at antique boat shows. And a contemporary incarnation of *Miss Columbia* built by Mark Mason for Philip Sharples — powered by an original Packard Gold Cup six — is the perennial favorite at the Thousand Islands Antique Boat Show in Clayton, New York. This is a story of passion and practicality.

Horace Elgin Dodge, Jr. saw his Dodge Boat Company reorganized as the Dodge Boat and Airplane Company. Even his great credibility and the financial strength stemming from his family's automotive success could not sustain the economic hemorrhage that resulted from his passion for the boat business. This is a story of business enabling art.

As much as this book is about the builders of the past, it is also about our contemporaries. The men and women who purchase, restore, and preserve these varnished artifacts from the past, often with as much disregard for practicality as their predecessors who designed, built, and raced them.

To these men and women, to everyone who has ever enjoyed an afternoon on the water, to anyone who appreciates history, fine craftsmanship, mahogany, metal and speed, this book is dedicated.

L I G H T N I N G 1

To folks of a practical mind, wooden boats in general and antique boats in particular don't have much to recommend. And even in the peculiar context of old wooden boats, James Woodruff's *Lightning* represents an extreme victory of history and aesthetics over practicality.

She's a drag-tail launch, designed and built in 1945 — along 1905 lines — at the Greavette boatworks under the supervision of Bert Hawker, who had been Ditchburn's designer from the mid-teens to the mid-1930s. Like *Miss Columbia*, she's a boat inspired by an engine. Her 1905 exposed-crankshaft, make-and-break ignition Standard Marine engine, with patents dating back to the 1890s, may be the last engine of this type in regular service.

Unlike contemporary engines, where ignition is provided by spark plugs (an improvement that achieved preeminence soon after *Lightning's* Standard was built), the spark in the Standard is generated by the collapse of a current that runs through a pair of small electrodes — the "igniter" — mounted in the side of the cylinder. Each cylinder has its own igniter, and at the appropriate moment a cam causes the two electrodes to part — the break — interrupting the flow of current and creating a spark. A make-and-break engine has no spark plugs or distributor.

Lightning is a legacy of Cameron Peck, the kind of affluent, obsessive collector that made the boats featured in this book possible. His reputation as a collector of cars — more than 600 during his lifetime, with as many as 275 on any given day — is rivaled only by his reputation as an entertainer. Peck, who made his fortune in the dairy business, bought an automobile dealership to display his collection of cars. His parties were

legend: he would empty the showroom and bring in a few of his favorite legendary automobiles, along with lavish amounts of champagne, for the benefit of a few hundred of his closest friends.

Lightning had her genesis in Peck's visit to Ravenscrag, the Eaton family cottage near Windmere on Lake Rosseau in Canada. While purchasing *Wanda III*, a 100 foot steamboat, to add to his collection, Peck spotted the 1905 Standard engine. He commissioned Bert Hawker, by then retired and working in a liquor store, to design and supervise the construction of *Lightning* specifically to suit the vintage Standard.

All of this boat's construction is authentic turn-of-the-century technique. The hull is mahogany and cedar, with copper rivets securing the planking on bent oak frames.

The boat sold at an auction of Peck's remaining collection in 1952 to Nelson Davis, whose cottage was on Chaynemac Island, Lake Muskoka, near Beaumaris in Ontario. *Lightning* was subsequently stored hanging from the rafters of the Davis boathouse. James Woodruff purchased the boat from Davis.

After purchasing *Lightning*, James set about restoration. Paul Dodington, affectionately known as the "Dippy Doctor" as a result of his work on "Dippys," the famous disappearing-propeller skiffs known as "Dispros" in the States, made a two-year project of the Standard engine. He restored it over the winters of '80-'81. Dodington waxes loquacious over the old Standard, and specifically on the subject of make-and-break engines. "These guys were really ingenious to come up with these things. We think all our stuff is 'high tech', but these engines were beautifully made. The Standard may be the first engine to have a control intended to advance the

spark as the speed of the engine increases.

"Spark plugs were known at the time, but the ignition system in a spark plug engine is high-tension. If it gets wet you're out of business. You can pour salt water all over a make-and-break engine and it will still run. Acadia, out in Nova Scotia, still builds a make-and-break engine the same as 1925."

During the winter of '83-'84, Ron Butson of Butson Boats restored *Lightning*'s woodwork, replacing almost all the planks below the water-line. Rob Haggar is responsible for *Lightning*'s

varnish, and Dukes in Port Carling did the engine installation and final work. In a very real way, *Lightning* reflects the personality of James Woodruff. A past Commodore of the Muskoka Lakes Association, and descendant of a family whose cottage, Wimur Lodge, represents the best of the Muskoka Lakes tradition, James, and his small collection of antique boats, *Lightning* and *Dix*, is characterized by the phrase "Quality, not Quantity."

James never does anything the easy way, and owning and running *Lightning* is a case in point. The starting procedure: fill the oil reservoir in the transmission; fill the primary oil reservoir and oil-feed lines; lubricate and oil the crankshaft and camshaft; switch the ignition system to the battery; prime the cylinders through the small petcocks on top of the head. Finally, bend over, take a firm grasp of the starting crank, and pull briskly on the crank until she catches. When she catches, switch the ignition from the battery and Edison coil, which are used only for starting, to the magneto.

When James's efforts are rewarded with ignition, all of this is accompanied by a great deal of shaking, thumping, huffing and chugging. The crankshaft cranks, the connecting rods do their peripatetic dance and *Lightning* pulls away from the dock on her next adventure in an antique cloud of exhaust. Despite *Lightning*'s obvious elegance, James is probably not often accompanied by his girlfriend for a leisurely cocktail cruise. With a total-loss lubrication system, oil that doesn't reach the small pan beneath Standard's crankshaft is splattered along *Lightning*'s hull and bilges. Or over *Lightning*'s intrepid pilot.

True style has its price. Still, there's little doubt that in the case of *Lightning* the cost, in terms of involvement and commitment, is worth the reward. A rare engine, a beautiful boat, the preservation of 90 year-old boating history.

V I K I N G

2

U p in the village of Center Harbor on Lake Winnipesaukee, next to the public boat launch, there's a couple of old boat houses that look like they date from the turn of the century. In one is *Baby Bootlegger*; in the other is Bob Valpey's 1910 launch *Viking*. In every way that *Baby Bootlegger* is the consummate Gold Cup racing boat, *Viking* is the epitome of the authentic early launch.

Legend has it that Dr. Erickson, of New Hampshire's Squam Lake, while on vacation in the lands of his ancestors was smitten by the beauty of the traditional vessels of the fjords. Erickson returned with a set of plans. *Viking* was built from these Norwegian plans by the Perkins Boat Shop.

As every artist knows, it's a long step from concept to execution, and Perkins was forced to abbreviate the original design. The plans were for a 40 footer, but because the Perkins shop was only 35 feet in length, *Viking* lost seven feet amidships, making her 33 feet stem to stern... which doesn't seem to have diminished her performance an inch.

Strong and sound, with a swept-back stem, *Viking* is true to her heritage. With a soft chine, she's a severe roller; but she's a long-keeled straight runner, and fast.

Like her hull, the one-off product of a small local boatwright, *Viking's* original power — two twin-cylinder, two-cycle McDuff engines — pre-dates the uniformity of mass production. In a happy testimony to long use, *Viking's* McDuffs were replaced in 1932 with a six-cylinder Gray 88, which in turn was replaced by Bob Valpey in 1987 with a six-cylinder Palmer, a marine conversion of a 120 horsepower International Harvester engine.

Bob Valpey's approach is typical of those most committed to antique wooden boating: "I am only the custodian of the *Viking*," he defers.

"My family had a small cottage on Winnipesaukee, and beginning in 1937 we spent our summers there. I'm especially interested in launches. I was always impressed by the grace and ease with which they go through the water. Seeing these boats slide by, I thought them the

ultimate in finesse and beauty. *Viking's* condition speaks well of the quality of the workmanship and materials with which she was built."

Bob Valpey is *Viking's* third owner. After Dr. Erickson, she was owned by the Gregg family, whose son became the Governor of New Hampshire. In the traditional New Hampshire way, *Viking* was kept in the same boathouse, in Holderness, from 1910 to 1980 by all three owners.

When Valpey purchased her in 1972 she was structurally sound, but then underwent a "total cosmetic restoration." No more than three ribs were sistered.

An example of the mystery of the hull speeds of early launches, *Viking*, with her present power, can easily pass Winnipesaukee's landmark tourist excursion boat *Mt. Washington.*

True displacement vessels are limited in speed. At a given speed, which can be fairly accurately estimated on the basis of the length and beam of the boat, the hull creates an insurmountable bow wave. Additional power only causes the stern to squat down in an attempt to climb a self-created hill of water.

"*Viking's* about 27 miles per hour flat out," Valpey estimates. "She's embarrassingly economical; she burns less fuel than a five horse-

power outboard. And at 27 miles per hour the stern doesn't settle," the classic sign that a displacement hull is approaching the boat's built-in speed limitation.

It's a pretty good guess that there's some planing going on here. The hull must be getting out of the water and riding on top of it, instead of pushing through it. This in a boat that was designed in 1910 and based on the shape of a Norseman.

"I'm only the custodian of *Viking*," Valpey muses again.

"Hopefully the next guy will feel the same way."

C O M E   N   G O

3

Cliff Stanton, the current owner of *Come N Go*, suggests "his wife gave him the clock so he would get home on time from his fishing trips." The "him" in the story is William L. Mellon, chairman of Gulf Oil, Mellon as in "The" Mellons of Pittsburgh and the Mellon Bank, and a turn-of-the-century American cottager at Camp Vagabondia on Squirrel Island, Lake Muskoka, Ontario.

While there is some question as to whether *Come N Go* is the original name of this stately 38 foot product of her obsessively perfectionistic builder, Bert Minett, after 77 years on the Muskoka Lakes, the provenance of *Come N Go* is fairly well documented.

Stanton, of Brampton, Ontario and Tobin's Island on Lake Rosseau, purchased the boat from Charles Moon, who owned her for three years. Between 1950 and 1985 — until she was rescued by Moon —*Come N Go* gave yeoman service as a water taxi and tour boat for Beaumaris Marine. During the preceding year, *Come N Go* had been owned by the Hillman Family. All of which means that between 1915, when she was allegedly christened, and 1949, *Come N Go* made her home port at Camp Vagabondia on Squirrel Island, under the able and appreciative ownership of the Mellon family.

"I haven't been able to find *Come N Go* in the 1915 Muskoka Lakes boat registry," Stanton admits. And while some suggest that the boat's original name may have been *Vagabondia II* in

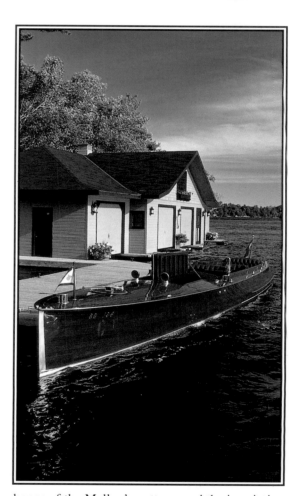

honor of the Mellon's cottage, and the inscription on the back of *Come N Go's* eight-day clock that Stanton received when he purchased the boat would substantiate the *Vagabondia II* legend,

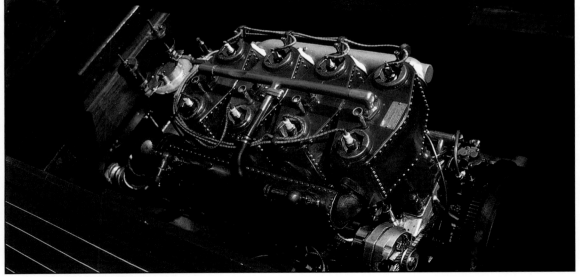

neither name is listed in the 1915 directory.

To muddy the waters further, when he had the hull varnished, Stanton found screw holes that fit perfectly with the nameplate mountings for *Come N Go*. Stanton isn't sure that the vintage Van Blerck engine he purchased and had installed in the boat is identical to her original engine but when he had the new Van Blerck mounted the screw holes also coincided, happily, with a set already there.

So it's all a little like translating the runes on an Egyptian pyramid.

Everett Macfarlane, who rebuilt the massive four-cylinder Van Blerck that powers *Come N Go*, suggests that the T-block design engine's manufacture dates from about 1911. A Canadian of Scottish descent, Macfarlane isn't given to exaggeration, but when he speaks of the Van Blerck one can hear the passion in his voice.

"It's a pretty thing," Macfarlane says. "Each cylinder was cast separately, and there's no separate head: the valves come out of brass ports in the top of each cylinder."

The cylinders are covered by gleaming brass plates, and "at one show," Macfarlane continues, "someone came by and suggested that the brass plates meant the engine had been repaired. Not so. That's the way she was made. There must be a thousand screw nails holding the brass plates on the sides of each cylinder."

In terms of complexity, *Come N Go's* Van Blerck rivals the 1905 Standard make-and-break engine that powers James Woodruff's *Lightning*. In the detailed manner of one who cares deeply about such things, Macfarlane describes the Van Blerck's lubrication: "The oiling is unique. The engine has a sump in the bottom of the crankcase. The oil is pumped from there to an oil container on the rear of the engine, and then another pump

powers the oil to the main bearings. It also fills troughs underneath the connecting rods, where dippers lubricate the connecting rods, which splash the cylinder walls and camshafts with oil."

"One of the toughest parts of the rebuild was adjusting the two oil pumps. The lower pump can't go so fast as to overflow the rear oil reservoir, but it has to go fast enough to keep up with the upper pump."

Macfarlane is reluctant to speculate on the horsepower of the Van Blerck, but, when pressed, he suggests 45 or 46 horsepower might be a rough guess. To the contemporary mechanic, this may seem small. Still, there are four immense long stroke cylinders here, and a total displace-ment of about 620 cubic inches, so those pretty brass plates conceal an engine of what can only be considered astronomic torque.

And about that clock.

"The Mellons had another, similar, Minett. Vintage 1915," Stanton says. "It's called the *Carry All* , and it's still over at Camp Vagabondia on Squirrel Island." Mellon's daughter, Margaret Mellon Hitchcock, still summers on Squirrel Island too, and "she's after that clock or my life," says Stanton.

"She says the clock wasn't part of the boat, and it still belongs with her family. We know that after the *Come N Go* was commissioned with her original Van Blerck, the Mellons had her repow-ered with two Packards, back to front, single screw. The boat has always been fast. She'll do 25 miles per hour now, with a 77 year-old racing engine. But she's a little hard to pilot, the engine really has no idle, and she wants to run.

"William Mellon had a picnic island, Blueberry Island, about 25 miles from Camp Vagabondia on Squirrel Island. And he liked to go fishing. Presumably he had a little skiff mounted on davits on the stern of *Come N Go*, and he'd fish from the skiff, somewhere around Blueberry Island. He could afford enough power to get home on time, but you know how wives are. He already had the faster engine, so his wife gave him a better clock."

When the four Ditchburn brothers, William, Henry, John and Arthur, emigrated in 1869 from England to Rosseau, they brought to the Ontario frontier a family tradition of boat building that dated back to the days of Queen Elizabeth I, Sir Francis Drake, and the Spanish Armada. Brother John Ditchburn left Rosseau for Toronto, but William and Arthur, and particularly Henry, turned their hands to the historic family trade. By 1874, when Pratt's Hotel in Rosseau had created a tourist demand for rowboats and canoes, the Ditchburns had a livery of 24 boats that they rented on a daily or weekly basis.

In 1890 the Ditchburns moved the boat business to Gravenhurst, and, according to A. H. Duke's *The Boatbuilders of Muskoka*, Henry Ditchburn is reputed to have built the first gasoline launch on the Muskoka lakes, in Gravenhurst in 1893.

Herb Ditchburn, Henry's nephew, joined the company sometime in the 1890s, and by 1898 the Ditchburns were committed to the business of building launches. In 1904 Herb took over, and by 1908 the company offered a full line of small craft, up to and including a 45 foot day cruiser.

Pausar, built in Gravenhurst over the winter of 1918, is a 30 foot six-inch Ditchburn launch that had the good fortune to be "discovered" in Magnetewan, Ontario, by H. A. "Pete" Laurence in 1986. "She had a tree growing over her deck and the branches had indented the bow.

Raccoons, squirrels and chipmunks had contributed to her indignity and she was filled with many years of autumn leaves. From what we know, she was first used as a family launch until about 1954, when she was pressed into livery

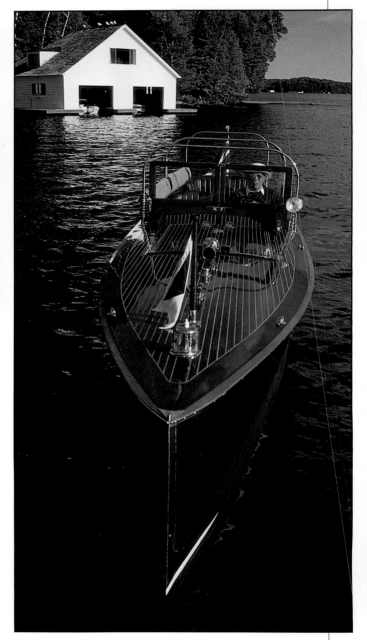

service as a water taxi. "Time passes quickly," Pete Laurence muses. "People have these old boats in the yard, and every year they say 'Well, next summer I'm going to fix her up,' but the summers are short... and they never do. And people just hate to part with a beloved old boat."

Pausar is a fairly standard Ditchburn launch from this era, but there were no blueprints. Ditchburn never built a boat without an order; they'd carve a half-model to show the lines, and get orders that way. Still, if you measured two boats that are supposedly identical they'd likely be a little different.

"Top speed is probably in the low twenties; you might be able to get her up to 25 miles per hour. *Pausar* is narrow, with a five-foot six-inch beam, and she runs a little wet, so it's most comfortable to cruise at about 18 miles per hour. Three years after *Pausar* was built, Ditchburn

widened his hulls by a foot and built them a plank higher, so they ran a little dryer."

The largest, most productive, and certainly the oldest of the early Muskoka boatbuilders, Ditchburn is believed by many to have been the best. Still, a high standard of quality provides no immunity from hard times. In 1930 Ditchburn had an impressive sales office in Toronto displaying a variety of launches offered through a wide price range. Ditchburn had built boats large and small for clients in the United States and across the vast expanse of Canada.

No matter.

On the 26th of May, 1932, Ditchburn was adjudged bankrupt. Like Dodge and Hacker, Ditchburn was to build boats under various other financial incarnations — until 1938 — but never to regain the productivity and prosperity of the first three innovative decades of the 20th century.

FAIRHAVEN 5

To those who spend time on the water, from the lowliest harbor rat to the most affluent owner, boats do seem to take on a life of their own. If you've worked in or around a harbor, you get to know the local vessels like old familiar friends. You may not know their owners; but you've probably heard of them, and if you're out at the islands and a local boat pulls into an adjacent bay, it always feels like good company has arrived.

For old-timers on Lake Winnipesaukee, Fairhaven is a good old friend.

The greybeards may remember her as Cranecrest, a spanky new 1920 wedding gift to Dr. Henry Crane, who owned this 20 foot Consolidated Laker until 1960, when she was sold to William Hunnewell, who made a home for her at the boathouse of "Fairhaven," his Meredith cottage. Sandy Fisken, William Hunnewell's daughter, and Fairhaven's present owner, inherited the boat in 1973.

"She was my father's pride and joy," Sandy remembers. "But when Dad died, to us she was just an old boat in the boathouse. We loved her, but Dad had done all the maintenance himself, and she was old and sort of undependable.

"We thought about taking out this old engine — a Universal 6 installed in 1926 — and replacing it with a Ford Mercury or something. But our son-in-law, Dick Kurth, is an electrical engineer, and in the summers he'd come up on the weekends and tinker with the old Universal.

"One weekend Dick yelled out that the had her running, so we all jumped in the boat in our bathing suits, the kids brought their sand toys, and we went for a cruise. The boat was dirty and the upholstery looked awful, but we had heard on

the radio that the Antique and Classic Boat Society was having a show of old boats. We said 'Let's see what the others look like,' and headed off for the Weirs.

"So we went by, and someone hailed us, and they tied us off and made great welcoming noises. But there was a $10 entry fee, and we were in our bathing suits — no money.

"Just at that moment a voice in the crowd shouted out 'Mr. Hunnewell?' It was Crane McCune, the grandson of Dr. Crane, who had sold the boat to my father. Crane recognized the boat, and offered to lend us the entry fee."

It must have been serendipity.

"The judges were wonderfully polite. The boat hadn't been dusted off, it was full of half-clad kids; the horn didn't work; the cockpit was covered with sand.

"But the judges acted as if we'd brought them a jewel.

"They advised us to keep the old Universal engine. We had the metal fittings re-nickeled; on boats this old it's nickel plating, not chrome. Slowly, year by year, we went through the whole boat restoring it. I think that's the whole value of the Antique and Classic Boat Society — members help other members.

"Now it's a great old boat."

Once again Fairhaven is a familiar sight on Winnipesaukee, and Sandy Fisken has become a familiar sight at ACBS gatherings. She just retired after four years as North East Chapter Secretary. If you ask her age, she'll smile and say "I'm seventy, and I'm proud of it. I was born the same year as the boat."

Serendipity.

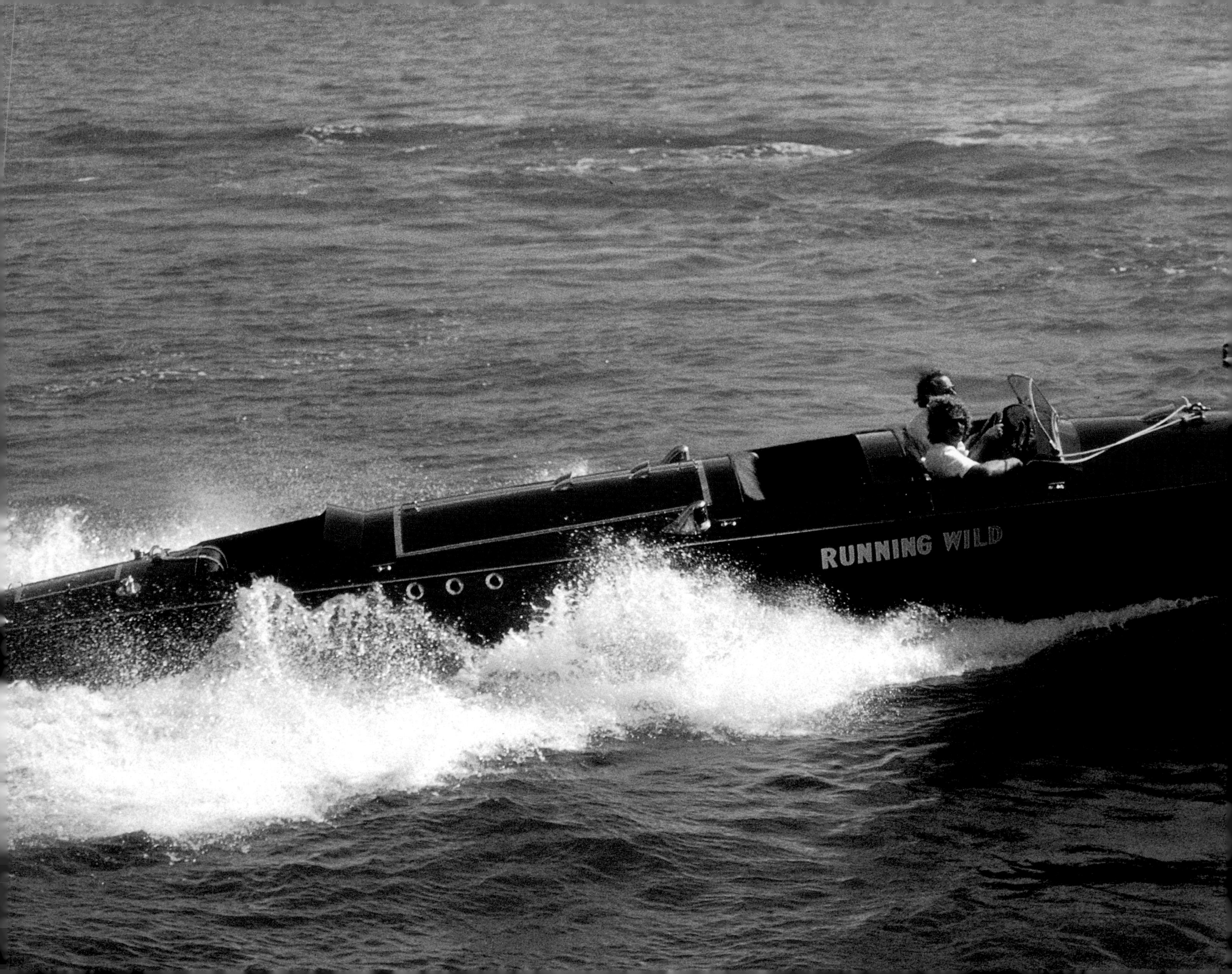
RUNNING WILD

RUNNING WILD

6

Before Chris Smith and Horace Dodge and John Hacker and Gar Wood did for power boating what Henry Ford did for the automobile — mass production of similar models with interchangeable parts — things were a little more complicated. Those who would go boating first commissioned a designer and then a builder (probably a local boatwright with few employees and a small shop) to create a vessel suited to the owner's particular needs and desires.

If the prospective owner was a wealthy industrialist with the urge to race, all the better. He could afford a first-class naval architect, a builder with an excellent reputation, quality materials and workmanship, and a power plant with enough *cojones* to match the competition. In the 'teens and 'twenties, and through the 'thirties, this often meant a V12 Liberty engine developed for the airplanes of World War I. This magic combination won races and created legendary boats — boats like *Running Wild*.

Thirty-one feet six-inches long, *Running Wild* is a triple-cockpit racing runabout built during the winter of '22-'23 by Francis "Roy" Stanley in Stanley's Cape Vincent boat shop in the Thousand Islands. The entire hull is batten-seam, copper-riveted construction, and powered by the equally legendary Gar Wood Liberty V12 conversion.

Since before the turn of the century, boats have been a way of life in the Thousand Islands (the locals will tell you there are actually closer to 1500 islands). Sometime around 1880 wealthy families discovered this summer haven, and island summer estates with expansive Victorian homes were built in places like Comfort Island, Dark Island and Heart Island with its Boldt Castle. For many the Thousand Islands were just a balmy place to escape the heat and stress of

urban summer living, but with the advent of power boating, those who could afford it, and probably a few that couldn't, fell victim to the seduction of speedboat racing. And perhaps they found the long summer days tedious, and just needed something to replace the excitement of big business deals.

We know that *Running Wild* was commissioned by Martin Shaughnessy, a wealthy industrialist with a summer home in Cape Vincent. She raced regularly on the St. Lawrence, taking part in local "Free For All" races, gala events sponsored by the respective Chambers of Commerce of St. Lawrence communities like Clayton, Cape Vincent and Alexandria Bay.

Newspaper clippings tell us *Running Wild* won several races in 1926; she had a tendency to trade trophies back and forth with *Snail*, another legendary boat, owned by Edward Noble who invented "Lifesaver" candies.

In the early twenties, any boat with Liberty power was fast, and although it isn't certain that her current engine is the original Liberty with which she was commissioned, she'll still leave almost everyone in her wake, running somewhere between 50 and 60 miles per hour.

Some suspect that the identity of the gifted designer who laid down *Running Wild's* lines 70 years ago is questionable. All indications, and the opinions of those with a mind for history and an eye for lines, suggest that *Running Wild* is a John Hacker creation. Dick Clarke of Sierra Boat, Mark Mason of New England Boat and Motor, and Don Price, proprietor of St. Lawrence Restoration (and *Running Wild's* owner since 1981), agree with other experts that *Running Wild* looks and performs like a product of John Hacker's drawing board. In confirmation, *Running Wild's* fittings are indeed vintage Hacker hardware.

Over 30 feet long, Liberty-powered, the unique product of both an inspired designer, John Hacker, and an exceptional local builder, Roy Stanley... and most importantly still on the water, *Running Wild* in the flesh brings power boat dreams and history alive.

RAINBOW IX 7

For the most part, the history of speedboat racing is a story about a small fraternity of driven men. Men of talent, creativity and foresight. Men of affluence who could afford to indulge a passion. And simple men who worked with their hands.

Often from the perspective of the present looking back at the past, one is tempted to identify a turning point, an epiphany, a moment in history when forces of personality or technological innovation combined to dramatically alter the course of future events.

Tolstoy would not have agreed. He viewed history and the course of human events as a continuum, with no single person, event, or time more important than any other. To Tolstoy, history was the movement of forces beyond human control. All was prelude, and the tendency to identify any single action or time as more important than another is just a symptom of the human need to organize, to make existence understandable, to create order out of chaos.

Tolstoy notwithstanding, seen from the perspective of the 1990s, 1922 was a year of epiphany in speedboat racing. The Gold Cup rules had changed. Chris Smith was no longer in partnership with Gar Wood. And Packard was to become a new and formidable power in speedboat racing engines.

Packard's Colonel Jesse G. Vincent, in a precedent-setting race, won the Gold Cup. Racing for the first time under new rules, Vincent piloted *Packard Chriscraft*, the first boat to bear the Chris-Craft name, albeit not hyphenated.

In an innovative move Vincent, the chief of engineering for Packard, had removed six cylinders of a 12 cylinder Packard engine in order to comply with hastily adopted engine-displacement restrictions.

Although it was the ninth consecutive Gold Cup victory for Chris Smith-built hulls, it was the first victory for Chris-Craft, and brought to an end a string of five consecutive victories by Gar Wood-driven boats.

There were 19 Smith-designed boats in the race. The winning *Packard Chriscraft* is said to be the hull on which successive thousands of Chris-Craft runabouts were based.

The historical evidence is that *Rainbow IX* is the victorious *Packard Chriscraft*, one of at least four hulls built by Smith for Jessie Vincent. In addition to the original *Packard Chriscraft*, the other three were *Miss Packard*, *Packard Chriscraft II*, and *Packard Chriscraft III*.

It was the first Gold Cup victory for Colonel Vincent, who went on to win again in 1923. But Vincent's 1922 Gold Cup, and even his 1923 Gold Cup, pale in comparison to a lifetime of accomplishments in a variety of endeavors that

probably would not be possible in today's era of specialization.

Colonel Jesse G. Vincent co-designed the Liberty Aircraft engine, the World War I power-plant which was and remains the engine of choice for twenties and thirties speedboats. Despite being self-educated, Vincent was Packard's chief engineer, a brilliant innovator who designed racing and production automobiles and managed Packard engineering for four decades.

Following the 1922 Gold Cup victory, Packard designed and produced a purpose-built Packard Gold Cup 6 that featured four valves per cylinder, a piece of sophisticated engineering that finally found its way into production automobiles

in the late 1980s. It's a pretty good bet that Colonel Vincent was at least in part responsible for this engine that dominated the Gold Cup for 15 years.

If 1922 marked a year of accomplishment for Jesse Vincent, it marked the end of a long and productive relationship between two of speedboat racing's giants.

Soon after Baldy Ryan, Chris Smith's original patron and racing collaborator, dissipated his fortune and disappeared from the racing scene, Chris Smith established with Gar Wood the boat-building and racing partnership that was responsible for Gar Wood's five Gold Cup victories. Gar Wood financed, Napoleon Lisee and Chris Smith designed and built, and Gar Wood drove the fastest boats of the times.

One suspects that at first Gar Wood's personality was complementary to that of Chris Smith. Smith was easygoing and Wood was competitive and demanding. But the attraction of

opposites is often short-lived, and when Wood and Smith dissolved their partnership they became competitors in both racing and the boat-building business.

Gar Wood drove a Chris Smith hull in the 1922 Gold Cup, and although sources suggest that all the Chris Smith hulls in the race were identical, Wood was embittered, thinking that Smith had designed a superior hull for Vincent. An era of Wood–Smith collaboration was over.

Packard Chriscraft, already a catalyst of conflict that shaped the lives of speedboat racing's most influential men, in 1934 passed into the racing stable of Harry B. Greening. Commodore Greening was a Muskoka-area Canadian sportsman and racing challenger who matched and sometimes defeated America's fastest. Greening's *Rainbows*, many built by Ditchburn, were regular and formidable challengers for the most prestigious cups and trophies both north and south of the border.

Little remains of the original *Packard Chriscraft*. Over the years the boat has been modified to accept a number of power plants. When Greening purchased her she was Liberty-powered. Most recently she was modified to allow the installation of a contemporary 650 horsepower Italian BRM engine.

No matter. Throughout the brief history of racing, boats have been changed to suit the times. And in performance her pedigree is obvious. "She's the best riding boat I've ever driven," according to Muskokan Jack Buwalda, the owner of Beaumaris Marine. "You could put 1000 horsepower in her and she would handle it."

Some question the accuracy of *Rainbow IX's* provenance. They criticize modifications. They claim she's not the boat that won the Gold Cup. Others say that Canadian newspaper photographs from the 1930s show the white-sided *Packard Chriscraft* with both the original G38 Gold Cup racing number and T-31, identifying the boat as a sweepstakes racer.

It's the kind of controversy that will fuel conversations at the yacht club bar well past the turn of the century, and it's entirely consistent with the history of the boat.

Perhaps it's not important. *Rainbow IX* is old, she's on the water, she's fast, and no one's proven she isn't Jesse Vincent's winner. She's a boat entwined in the lives of four of speedboat racing's greats: Harry B. Greening, Gar Wood, Christopher Columbus Smith, and Colonel Jesse G. Vincent.

And attitudes have changed. Everything's more serious now. It wasn't always that way. As Mrs. Allen Flye, Harry Greening's granddaughter, remembers, "They didn't take themselves too seriously. They seemed to end up laughing at their misfortune. They seemed to have more fun."

M A X I N E

To even the most conscientious, history is often some slight movement at the periphery of one's vision, a brief glimpse, an unsubstantiated memory, some passing form viewed between the swells on the waters of time.

Opinions are many, facts are few. Was it all a dream?

For Stan Olsen, the owner of *Maxine*, this is the "known" history of his 33 1/2-foot displacement cruiser.

In 1928 John and Maxine Heath purchased *Maxine* for their honeymoon cruise on the Detroit River. A few nights after their marriage, while they were sleeping on board, an unidentified intruder boarded the vessel. John went on deck, wrestled with the intruder, and both John Heath and the intruder fell into the water. A short while later John returned to the boat.

A week after the incident, the body of a U.S. Customs agent floated to the surface of the Detroit River. U.S. Customs confiscated *Maxine* and she was stored in a boatyard somewhere in or near Detroit.

John Heath was arrested, charged with murder, and subsequently tried twice. Heath was acquitted at both trials. In 1938 or 1939, Henry Ford, or a representative of the Henry Ford Museum in Greenfield, Michigan, purchased the boat. She was completely restored and put on display at the Henry Ford Museum as a classic Rum Runner. *Maxine* remained at the Ford Museum until 1984, when she was purchased by Michael

Matheson of Murphy, North Carolina and Mt. Dora, Florida.

Five years later, in 1989, Stan Olsen purchased the boat from Michael Matheson. Gary

Scherb, of the Old Time Boat Company of Sarasota, Florida began a six-month restoration and in July of 1990 *Maxine* returned to the water for the first time since 1928. At the North East Chapter Antique and Classic Boat Society Show on Lake Winnipesaukee in 1990, *Maxine's* provenance, authenticity, and restoration were good enough to win her Best of Show.

What does Stan Olsen think?

"The Ford Museum says she was built in 1923; but she's powered by an in-line six-cylinder 1917 Kermath engine, and her fixtures seem

to date from 1917. We believe she was built in 1917. Because she was restored by the Ford Museum, when we got her everything was original, or original replacement.

"I'm amazed at the handling and hull design. She turns quickly, and she's not at all tender. I don't think we've improved hull design much since then. A true displacement hull, she rides like a sailboat under power, with a hull speed of about six or seven knots."

And the Heath mystery?

Stan Olsen says, "I think she might have been a rumrunner before Heath bought her. The U.S. government believed the boat was smuggling booze from Canada in burlap sacks tied to the keel."

Desperate men in fast boats remains the popular image of the Rum Runner, and on the Atlantic seaboard this was probably true. Some of the best Prohibition-era boat designers drew plans euphemistically titled "Fast Fisherman" or "Express Freight" vessels, to be powered by one or more Liberty engines, and intended to outrun the pathetically undermanned Coast Guard blockade defending the sobriety of U.S. shores. But this may not have been where the real action was.

Vintage estimates suggest that in 1923 25,000 smugglers were bringing 100,000 gallons a day across the Detroit River. By 1928 Detroit was termed the "Rum Capitol of the Nation." And there's little doubt that along the Detroit River, and along the length of the St. Lawrence, stealth — not speed — was the chief ally of the smuggler.

So Stan Olsen's probably right. "The Rum Runners weren't all that fast," he says. "They went under cover of darkness. I believe *Maxine* is a classic Rum Runner."

Or was it all a dream?

BABY BOOTLEGGER 9

I
t's a grey dawn on Lake Winnipesaukee; a mist on the water shrouds the tree-lined shores. Mark Mason throttles back on *Will-O-the-Wisp*, an elegant 30 foot Hacker, and the fenders gently kiss the dock at Center Harbor in a perfect landing.

It's not quite 6:30 AM, and the crew is still chasing the cobwebs with a thermos of coffee provided by photojournalist and first mate "Unsinkable" Polly Brown.

Mist or not, there's early morning electricity in the air.

Behind the doors of an unimpressive boathouse hides *Baby Bootlegger*. She of infamous, rounded sheer beauty and Hispano-Suiza power, two-time Gold Cup winner, once thought lost forever, snatched from the junkyard, resurrected, a boat to die for.

The doors open slowly, and the boathouse gloom recedes, shadows giving way to light. Sixty thousand varnished bronze plank fasteners speak to lifetimes of 1924 Nevins craftsmanship. On the bow, in gold leaf, a boxy almost childlike "G" and massive "5" shout "Gold Cup." There's not a whisper of the obsessive quest and restoration that brought *Baby Bootlegger* from her ignoble interment in an anonymous Quebec City junkyard.

This is the restorer's Art. A boat as she was, is, and ever shall be. No need to sign the work. No crass showmanship. Strictly business, like Shakespeare knocking out plays.

This is a boat, nothing more and nothing

less, age and speed and beauty notwithstanding, and Mark Mason climbs aboard and pulls the tackle chain, lowering *Baby Bootlegger*'s hull

into the boathouse waters. The hatch covers are opened, volatile gasoline fumes vented, and Mason fires the Hisso off.

She coughs, sputters, catches, dies.

Again.

The Hisso catches, a few cylinders, enough, and slowly all remaining cylinders sing in symphony. Exhaust fouls the boathouse air. When she's warm, Mason backs her out, crew at-the-ready to fend the boathouse corners. But Mason's confident, and all 30 feet clear the dock, the narrow 5' 8" beam safe now on the open waters of Winnipesaukee.

For George F. Crouch, *Baby Bootlegger*'s designer, 1924 was a vintage year. With three boats in the running, *Baby Bootlegger*, the Columbia Yacht Club's *Miss Columbia*, and Harry Greening's *Rainbow IV*, the Gold Challenge Cup Race was a showcase of Crouch designs.

Greening's *Rainbow IV* was the winner, disqualified under protest after the race by virtue of her twelve small transverse steps, which had been outlawed under the new "Gentleman's Raceboat" rules. And with *Rainbow*'s disqualification, *Baby Bootlegger*'s owner, millionaire, race-car driver, pilot, industrialist Caleb Bragg took home the Cup. Charles F. Chapman and his CYC syndicate had the small consolation of finishing officially second in *Miss Columbia*.

If the Gold Cup were horse racing, perhaps Crouch's designs would have been considered an "Entry," with all three boats racing under one flag. There's no question that each of these boats reflects Crouch's interpretation of each owner's desires. A quick look at *Miss Columbia* will confirm her more orthodox lines — she looks like "a boat" — and antique photos of *Rainbow* confirm her Canadian heritage; smooth and clean

and fastest she may have been, but the characteristic "monkey rails" say Muskoka Lakes loud and clear.

Baby Bootlegger, then, is perhaps a clue to Caleb Bragg's personality. Her rounded gunwales and unorthodox lines hide not for a second her muscularity: in every way that *Miss Columbia* is intellectual, discreet, traditional-yachting New York, *Baby Bootlegger* is strong and practical and beautifully vulgar and, to match her name, outside the law.

So three boats motor over to the Wiers and the 1990 ACBS Winnipesaukee show. In leather aviator's goggles Mark Mason pilots *Baby Bootlegger*, flashing by the photo boat, *Will-O-the-Wisp* — Polly Brown at the helm — while *Viking*, stabled next to *Bootlegger* in Center Harbor, takes an early lead, hoping not to be left behind by the faster boats.

Mason pulls up to the show docks, and curious eyes follow *Baby Bootlegger* — she's probably the most desirable antique speedboat in the world, after all. But there aren't a lot of oohs and ahs. *Bootlegger's* a Winnipesaukee regular — she's won "Best of Show," all there is to win — and almost everyone knows Mark. Plenty of the nation's hottest antique boats have been through his Laconia restoration shop, New England Boat and Motor.

So there's no competition. *Baby Bootlegger's* not entered in the show; she's just there on display, a great old boat to share with those who care about old boats.

A couple of days later the crew is sunning on the dock at the camp, enjoying a Winnipesaukee island afternoon, and someone is dying for a cruise in *Baby Bootlegger*. And the photographer wouldn't mind shooting a couple more rolls with blue skies.

Under clear skies at Center Harbor *Baby Bootlegger* is unveiled again, and a grinning Dick Hopgood — owner of the 28 foot Gar Wood *Bunco* — slides into the riding mechanic's seat next to Mark Mason. The photographer clambers into the regulation passenger's seat — if one can call it a seat — in the bow.

Baby Bootlegger is slapping across the late-afternoon Winnipesaukee wavelets at about 60, and forget about photography. It's a matter of survival: a combination of mortal terror and life's ultimate thrill. Of course, no one really rode in the passenger's seat for the Gold Cup; and, given the invitation, the photographer would do it again in a second, even if he did have to forget about photographs and cradle the camera in his lap, praying they would both survive.

This is what these old boats are about. Something few feel in life. Not just an appreciation of beauty, but also a shared experience, a spanning of generations. Riding in the boat that won the 1924 and 1925 Gold Challenge Cups. Is this how Caleb Bragg felt, full out, in three thirty-mile heats of the run for the Gold?

Who can say? Caleb Bragg was too busy flying, racing, and industrializing to write about it.

And still, a voice from the past remains. Mrs. R. B. Timberlake who, along with her husband, docked *Baby Bootlegger* at the Timberlake's St. Lawrence boathouse out of Montreal from 1927 to 1947, is quoted in Mason Smith's *WoodenBoat* story:

"It was very avant-garde for a woman to drive a speedboat in the twenties. I'd say to Tim, 'Let's go for a boat ride.' He'd say 'We have no fuel,' I'd say, 'Stay right there and read your paper. I'll take the chauffeur and go to the airport.' We'd go to the airport, strap on two huge cans of gas. And there I was, driving a bomb down the road, just so my husband would give me a ride in the *Baby Bootlegger*.

"You know when you're in an airplane, and the engines are fired up, and the whole plane trembles, and with a great thrilling frightening roar you run down the airstrip, and you feel that this is absurd, this thing can't fly, and then you take off! That's the feeling I got with every ride in *Baby Bootlegger*.

"When we went out on the water and warmed the engine up, and then ran up the river, we'd round the lighthouse and come back at high speed. And all the people in the clubhouse — the bar, the dining room — would have got up and gone down to the dock, and they'd be standing there waving and cheering as we passed."

MISS
COLUMBIA

10

hen the American Power Boat Association — then dominated by members of the Columbia Yacht Club of New York — initiated the Gold Challenge Cup Race in 1904, they established what was to become the world's premier power-boat race series. For ninety flat-out miles, with each boat racing in three successive thirty-mile heats, the Gold Cup evolved into a race that favored boats with one or more immense fire-breathing engines, many of them marine conversions of aircraft engines. Gold Cup winners were boats of subtle design and light construction, driven by daredevil pilots who cared more for winning races than living long enough to retire to a rocking chair. Although the first two decades of Gold Cup competition saw occasional victories for boats flying the Columbia Yacht Club burgee, by the early 1920s the boys at the CYC felt that the trophy was spending "way too much time" over mantlepieces in the Midwest, won by Gar Wood and his neighbors.

Every successive year the intensity of Gold

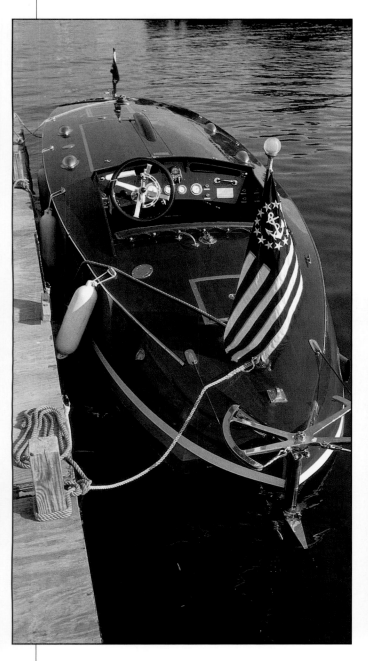

Cup competition necessitated new boats with bigger engines. As the boats had no other use, owners lost interest until in 1921 the class had almost become extinct. Only two boats were entered in competition that year.

For 1922 new Gold Cup rules were instituted. Boats were required to be of such a design that they would be useful for pleasure when not racing. The new "Gentleman's Raceboat" rules required a decked boat, a single engine limited to 625 cubic inches, a marine clutch with reverse gear, a water-cooled exhaust to the stern, and seating for at least four passengers. Within two years there were 20 boats entered in the race.

In 1923 a group of Columbia Yacht Club members formed a syndicate to build and race a boat that would bring the trophy home. Among the syndicate members was Charles F. Chapman, the editor and publisher of *Motor Boating* magazine for 48 years, one of the organizers of the U.S. Power Squadrons, and the author of *Piloting, Seamanship and Small Boat Handling* — still the definitive handbook for small-boat operators.

In December of 1923, the syndicate commissioned marine architect George Crouch to design *Miss Columbia*, and by July of 1924 boatwright Henry B. Nevins and the CYC launched a 27-foot boat of surpassing beauty. She raced for the first time that same month, with Chapman at the helm.

During her first year of competition *Miss*

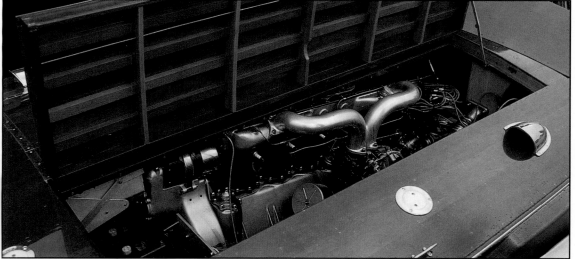

Columbia was powered by a 625 cubic-inch Wright Gold Cup marine conversion of a Hispano-Suiza aircraft engine. The flush woodwork of her bow concealed a small cockpit, ostensibly to provide seating for two passengers, in addition to the stern seating for the driver and mechanic who raced her. A double-ender, she featured a stern rudder controlled by a massive steering quadrant of sculptural beauty.

Like many of the Gold Cup racers of her era, *Miss Columbia* went through various incarnations. In 1925 she was repowered with a 621 cubic-inch six created for the Gold Cup Class by the Packard Aircraft Company. She ran the rest of her career with that engine.

When the rules were changed to allow hydroplanes in the 1929 race, six small steps were built into her hull, accompanied by air vent tubes behind each step to permit air to fill the vacuum created by the steps, thus smoothing water flow. Toward the end of her career, she raced under the colors of the Red Bank Yacht Club in New Jersey.

A perennial bridesmaid, *Miss Columbia* never did win the Gold Cup, although she earned a reputation as the boat to finish second more than any other. Some believe that this is the result of Chapman's conservatism — he had too much respect for his boat to drive her to the very limit. He rarely blew up engines.

The final disposition of the original *Miss Columbia* is unknown, lost in the mist of history. But thanks to owner Phil Sharples, of the Thousand Islands, and restorer Mark Mason, who supervised the project, we now have a contemporary incarnation of *Miss Columbia*.

Wooden boat purists love to anguish over authenticity; but authenticity is rarely a clear-cut issue. Even the best preserved antiques have hull planks replaced. To many of the *cognoscenti*, wooden hulls are seen as analagous to the tires on a car — with use and age they wear out. Since use and enjoyment represent the essence of wooden-boat ownership, replacement should be no great cause for alarm.

In truth, the current *Miss Columbia* has more in common with a restoration than she does with a reproduction or replica. Her impressive Packard Gold Cup Six engine is identical to the Packard six that powered her famous predecessor. And the current engine is of legitimate historic provenance: it originally belonged to Horace Dodge, and powered his *Delphine IV* when she won the Gold Cup in 1932.

Miss Columbia's hull, built by Bill Cooper and Son, of Sippewissett, Massachusetts, conforms perfectly to the lines of the original *Miss Columbia*. The steering quadrant — cast, milled and plated nickel over bronze — is, like the hull, straight from George Crouch's original drawings. And her instruments are authentic U.S. Gauge instruments, with beveled glass lenses set in milled solid-brass cases, the result of an almost mythical quest by Mark Mason.

Visually indistinguishable from her namesake, Sharples' *Miss Columbia* sounds the same and undoubtedly handles the same on the water. Which is to say superlatively. Authenticity becomes a moot point.

When Philip Sharples fires up the big Packard, the six behemoth cylinders bark and blast. As he pushes the throttle forward, the wind and G-forces distort his cheeks as *Miss Columbia* slides and slices the St. Lawrence River round a point in the Thousand Islands. And if he should briefly glimpse Gar Wood — or Caleb Bragg — through the spray off the stern quarter, threatening to pass, who would say it's only imagination?

JAVELIN & SHELIZALOU 11

I n the lives of men, fate more often than not intervenes in some seemingly capricious manner, changing one's path, guiding the way, one apparently small step determining the next until in the context of history what began as a short walk becomes a lifetime journey with a discernible beginning, a middle, and an ending.

Fay & Bowen began in 1900 as a small upstate New York firm that manufactured spokes and nipples for bicycle wheels. Walter C. Fay was the business-oriented partner and Ernest S. Bowen was an engineer interested in the internal combustion engine.

Fay & Bowen wanted to build and market internal combustion engines. But at the turn of the century America's streets and roads ranged from bad to non-existent; the automobile was a product of unproven appeal, and it was the sentiment of many that the appropriate motive force for land-bound vehicles would always be living horse power.

William C. Smith, a Morristown, New Jersey restorer of boats and automobiles and the accepted authority on Fay & Bowen, suggests that in or around 1903 the gentle hand of fate intervened in the form of two circumstances. "Because the roads were bad, and Fay & Bowen discovered they had in their employ a man who knew how to build boats, the resources of the company were directed toward the building of boats."

The first documented Fay & Bowen was

built in 1903, and took the form of a fantail launch, similar in appearance to the steam and naptha launches that preceded it. By 1905 Fay & Bowen moved their base of operations from Auburn, New York to Geneva on the Finger Lakes.

Subsequent Fay & Bowen designs included a "torpedo-stern" model, a "special," numerous launches, and three boats: the "Junior 24," the "Runabout 27," and the "Golden Arrow," all of which were considered to be runabouts. *Javelin* and *Shelizalou* are both examples of the "Runabout 27," although to the modern eye they are obviously launches, dignified and elegant and all that the term "fast launch" implies, including ample cockpit space for wicker chairs and a speed range more civilized than thrilling.

As is so often the case, the seeds of our demise are planted in our early success. Walter Fay and Ernest Bowen, who captured the spirit of their times, were reluctant to give up their semi-displacement launches and fill the demand for the new sensation of the 1920s, the new planing-hull runabout.

Between 1903 and 1929 Fay & Bowen produced an estimated 900 boats; currently, 165 surviving Fay & Bowen small craft have been documented. The Fay & Bowen Engine Company was officially dissolved on February 25, 1929, more a victim of changing times than of economic disasters that were eight months in the future.

One hesitates to suggest that the Fay & Bowen launch, an American boat to match the Canadian Ditchburns and Minetts in simplicity and elegance if not in craftsmanship (nothing matches Canadian boats in craftsmanship), is an accident of fate. Still, William C. Smith contends that Fay & Bowen "built boats to prove an engine, rather than design a hull." Here we have two of them:

Hull #770, *Javelin* was built in 1925 and shipped by rail in the Spring of 1926 to her first owner, who was the head chef at the Saranac Inn on Lake Saranac, New York. Sometime around 1930 she was repowered with a 60 horsepower

Universal six, her current power plant. It has been suggested that *Javelin* spent time on Lake Placid, New York during the 1960s. Not always purely a pleasure vessel, she has been a mail boat and an excursion vessel. Bill Munro, who restored *Javelin*, found her in the barns adjoining the Saranac Inn in 1987.

Hull #739, *Shelizalou* was built in either 1924 or 1925. Little is known of her history, with the exception of the fact that at some time she was caught in a storm on Lake George, New York, and sank at her mooring. Mark Mason of New England Boat and Motor restored her for Carl Best, her current owner. *Shelizalou's* new home port is Homewood, on Lake Tahoe. She's powered by a Scripps six-cylinder engine.

JAVELIN

CHALLENGER 12

At the Sierra Boat Company of Carnelian Bay on Lake Tahoe, in symbolic deference to the long hours of craftsmanship that skilled woodworkers and mechanics spend on each restoration, the boat's owner takes possession only after the craftsmen have delivered the finished product — in a ritual maiden voyage — to the annual Tahoe Yacht Club *Concours d'Elegance.*

After the show the new owner, totally unfamiliar with his boat, is faced with the prospect of backing something polished and perfect out of the cramped dock space of the Tahoe Boat Company marina.

So when *Challenger's* owner Doug Elmore confesses, "I was terrified to drive her!" it is less an admission of timidity than a statement of good sense.

Challenger is not only one of Gar Wood's first "Baby Gars" — and one can only view "Baby" as an immodest misnomer for a 33 foot Liberty-powered gentleman's raceboat — but she's also overpowered, designed to go fast, mainly in straight lines, and a boat of true historic import: only a handful of "Baby Gars" have survived the ravages of time.

For skippers of contemporary small craft, spoiled by the convenience of the outdrive which swings the prop in a radius off the stern, backing down is no great challenge. Modern boats back straight and true.

But single-prop inboards — traditional boats

— are a different matter. The rotation of the prop creates torque that causes the stern to "prop walk" when backing, either to port or starboard, depending in which direction the prop turns.

Backing down becomes an art, best applied after more than one practice docking, hopefully under flat water conditions and in an unobstructed area.

At the 1990 Tahoe Yacht Club Show, Doug Elmore, an experienced skipper, joined an elite fraternity of antique boat owners whose first turn at the helm is in full view of the thrill-loving crowd at the *Concours*.

It is a magic moment.

The show is over. A warm glow permeates the crowd.

Proud owners and their crews prepare to cast off, and first one and then another Liberty engine fires off. A deafening counterpoint of twelve-cylinder engines in competing glory fills the air.

Crew, owners, and dockside bystanders are at-the-ready to fend off. There's no blood-lust here. These boats are too delicate and too valuable for anyone to take pleasure in a crunch.

After much jockeying, backing-down, swinging of sterns, and more than a couple of near cardiac arrests, a proud procession of some of the finest boats in the hundred-year history of speedboating parades through the narrow breakwater gate of the Tahoe Boat Company marina.

In 1990, and despite Doug Elmore's trepidation, *Challenger* was the proudest of them all. Best of Show, First in Class, armfuls of trophies went to *Challenger* and Doug Elmore at the presentation picnic Sunday afternoon.

And rightly so. *Challenger* is a boat of proud provenance and historic importance, restored by some of the most skilled craftsmen in the field, and owned by a man whose pleasure is derived more from the preservation and enjoyment of great old boats than in acquisition and ostentation.

With the possible exception of the few remaining Gold Cup racers, a 33 foot "Baby Gar"

is the pride of any antique speedboat fleet. She's a direct descendant of Gar Wood's *Baby Gar IV*, the boat in which Wood challenged the Twentieth Century Limited in a legendary 1925 race. Crowds watched as the boat raced the express train on a New York-to-Albany run and saw the Hudson River-bound speedboat beat the prestigious Twentieth Century Limited by 17 minutes. It was a typical Gar Wood — and typical twenties — performance.

The decade between the Great War and the Great Depression was in love with the idea of speed and recklessness and adventure, and Gar Wood's race was emblematic of the fervor of the times. The media-generated enthusiasm resulted in impassioned pleas from the adventurous rich for Gar Wood to duplicate his boat in a form that they could enjoy. Thus the "Baby Gar."

Eventually the "Baby Gar" was to become a production boat, albeit produced in limited quantities. But *Challenger*, commissioned in 1926 by the Philip Wrigley of chewing gum, Chicago Cubs, and Catalina Island fame, must have been one of the first of these boats in private hands.

Christened *Helen A*, in honor of Wrigley's sister, *Challenger* was rechristened by Doug Elmore. Arguments will persist *ad infinitum* between traditionalists, who believe it is bad luck to change the name of a boat, and new owners, who wish to change the identity of a boat to match their own personality. Maybe it's excusable. Perhaps if a boat is named after another man's sister, or sweetheart, or wife, dispensation may be made. Besides, *Challenger* had been the name of a legendary Lake Tahoe Gar Wood long disappeared from the lake's waters.

On the still, early morning Sierra water, an elite crew is gathered. The unlikely photo boat is

Steve Lapkin's *Aurora*, a rare Canadian Barnes launch. Tony Brown, restorer *extraordinaire* and *concours* judge, is switching from boat to boat, crewing where he is needed.

As for speed, *Aurora* is no match for *Challenger*. The photographer is burning film as *Challenger* roars by. Long and lean with at least the first twenty feet riding low but dry, the Liberty V12 thundering and Doug Elmore grinning like a kid on the first day of summer vacation, *Challenger* is an apparition from the past.

Challenger has a V-drive, a short drive shaft running towards the bow from the power take-off of the Liberty into a gearbox beneath the pilot's seat which turns the prop shaft. The rumble and vibration are a constant reminder of the barely restrained 500 horsepower beneath the 70 inch hatches astern. Because of the V-drive, the transmission lever is backwards: one pushes forward for reverse and backward to go forward.

Doug Elmore is, in the flattering sense of the word, a simple man. He's more than successful selling central California ranches, but one's impression is that he'd be successful at whatever he tried. He's a man who loves boats, but doesn't love them to show off. In a surprising admission, he'll tell you, "Well, Dick Clarke says, 'This is a boat that should be saved — and saved at Lake Tahoe,' and I buy it."

Almost *de facto*, Doug Elmore has one of the nicest small collections of old wooden boats in the nation. Because Dick Clarke said, "This is a boat that should be saved."

D I X

13

Legend suggests that this Ditchburn's unusual name, *Dix*, is a precocious contraction of Dick's, after Dick Clemson, *Dix's* youthful first owner. Dix was built when Dick Clemson was probably in his late teens. He was a young American from Philadelphia whose affluent family summered at their cottage near Beaumaris on Lake Muskoka.

A 21 foot 1927 Ditchburn Gentleman's Racer, *Dix* is a direct descendant of *Rainbow I*, built by Herb Ditchburn for Harry Greening, and of the Ditchburn racers *Whippet* and *B IV*.

The record books show that Clemson campaigned Dix in the late 1920s and early 1930s in local races at the Beaumaris Yacht Club and in the Balla Regatta in Balla, Ontario. The characteristic "monkey rails" on the deck along the gunwales are a common feature of Ditchburn racers, allowing the grease monkeys to horse the boat around at the dock during pit stops.

Cameron Peck spotted *Dix* at the Greavette shop in Gravenhurst in 1945, and the Peck boathouse on the Lake of Bays became the boat's new home. Peck replaced the original six-cylinder, twin-carb Scripps 76 Junior Gold Cup engine with a Buchanan Meteor.

In 1952 Nelson Davis, a wealthy Canadian financier, purchased *Dix* at an auction of Peck's collection of boats. In 1979 James Woodruff bought the boat from Davis, and commissioned a complete restoration. Duke Marine in Port Carling did the woodwork, which included a

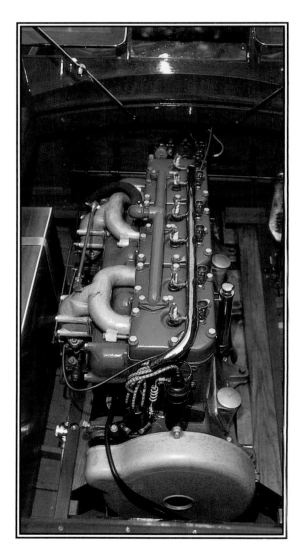

complete rebuild of the hull starting a couple of planks below the deck.

Parts from three cannibalized antique Scripps engines went into the Junior Gold Cup Six that now powers *Dix*. James Woodruff isn't a flashy guy, and there are probably a few Muskokans who think of him as a little bit of an organic character. Still, James wears his shades when he takes *Dix* out for a run. Must be the small windshield.

Sunglasses notwithstanding, Mr. James Woodruff is at least as traditional as anyone else in the northern reaches above the U.S. Who else would go to the trouble of finding, salvaging, and building a running power plant out of three antique 1920s six-cylinder Scripps Junior Gold Cup engines?

A-9

14

There is little doubt that during the first decades of speedboat racing one was much more likely to see the name of a woman on the transom of a boat than to see a woman at the helm. This was, after all, an era of launches piloted by liveried chauffeurs, when dignity was a responsibility of wealth and racing was left to thrill-seekers and, in general, those of dubious sanity.

Which is not to say that women went unrepresented. Or that women on the race course did not acquit themselves with at least as much honor and courage and determination as the male competitors.

Happily, speedboat racing is representative of the best of the industrial revolution. Inasmuch as the machine does most of the work, driving a race boat is more a matter of desire and courage, good judgment and an intimate knowledge of the boat's abilities, than strength. Women regularly attended the speedboat races, and not always as the loyal spouses or attractive guests on the judges' launch.

In particular, women were driving Class A hydroplanes, the 91 cubic-inch class. Betty Carstairs was a regular competitor in this class, when she wasn't racing her 35 foot triple Napier engine *Estelle IV* with its 3000 total horsepower against Gar Wood for the Harmsworth Trophy. And outboard racing champion Loretta Turnbull, who with regularity shamed the best of the competition, was there competing, with

Mary Crandell as her riding mechanic.

A-9 is not an antique boat. She was built in 1989-90 by Ralph Glass and John Clark. But she was built from plans for *Flyer*, a vintage 91

cubic-inch inboard racer that appeared in a 1927 issue of *Motor Boating* magazine. Her Fay & Bowen "Rocket" engine and all the hardware were salvaged from the original *Van Blerck Flyer* that was raced during the early thirties by Loretta Turnbull and Mary Crandell.

So it is no accident that a photo of Ms. Turnbull and Ms. Crandell slicing the chop is the lead illustration of the *Motor Boating* story that details the construction of this successful vintage speedster.

A-9's owner, John "Speedboy" Clark, a tall southerner with equal parts of abrasiveness and charm, is one of the true characters of antique boating. He's adventured everywhere and done everything, from Bangkok to Lexington. His antique boating credentials are impeccable. He's been down and out in New Mexico, and he's rubbed shoulders with the rich and famous as a horse breeder and trainer, most notably as assistant trainer for Seattle Slew.

Right now — and one's never sure where John's wanderlust will lead him — he's an antique-boat-engine freak. When he's not on the antique boat circuit, Florida to New Hampshire, he's in his "Bluegrass Boat and Motor" shop in Versailles, Kentucky, probably rebuilding some antique Van Blerck engine. He has no time for snobbery — or sycophants.

John Clark represents the best of antique boating. He won't tell you, but the evidence is that he's committed to individual effort, good work done well, whether it be rebuilding antique boat engines or training thoroughbred racehorses.

A-9 reflects John Clark's commitment, and here is what he has to say about her:

"Bruce N. Crandell designed the *Flye*r, and his brother Willard authored the *Motor Boating* article. Bruce and Willard Crandell were boat racers first and later were designers. They finally established the Crandell Boat Company, Newport Beach, California and, ultimately, another plant in Phelps, Wisconsin.

"*A-9's* woodwork, by Ralph Glass, is authentic. The plans and construction methods of the era were strictly adhered to. We used the hardware and engine from an original Crandell boat, the *Van Blerck Flyer*."

The 91 cubic-inch Class designation may seem arbitrary in cubic inches, but it reflects the international nature of the class. In America, these boats raced with the "A" prefix on their hull numbers: In Europe, where 91 cubic inches translates to a 1.5 liter Class, the boats raced with the "Z" prefix.

"The class was popular on both sides of the Atlantic. Carl G. Fisher, Harry B. Greening, D.P. Davis, Charles Chapman, Betty Carstairs, Ralph Snoddy and even the famous Garfield Arthur Wood competed regularly," John Clark tells us.

So when one sees an antique photo of a small race boat with both an "A" and a "Z" number, the underlying message is that this is an international boat.

In one of those moves designed to confuse even the most conscientious boat historian, the engine in the original *Van Blerck Flyer* was not, in the most accurate sense, a Van Blerck. The engine is in fact a Fay & Bowen "Rocket," an engine of Van Blerck manufacture, virtually indistinguishable from the same engine that carried the Van Blerck name, but originally sold by the famous Fay & Bowen boatworks of Geneva, New York.

It may seem sad, but it is the way of the world that many great things are self-limiting, perhaps especially racing classes of boats. The popularity of the 91 cubic-inch Class eventually drew the attention of Harry Miller, the jeweler of engine builders, and he designed and built a 1.5 liter straight-eight marine engine to race in this class.

The Miller engine was far superior, and the choice for 91 class competitors was to acquire a Miller engine at great expense or retire and compete in another more affordable class. Attempts were made — limitations on construction and engine costs, primarily — to extend the life of the class. And rightly so. These boats are modest in size, but at least as thrilling as anything else on the water.

Still, by the mid-thirties there were greater satisfactions to be found elsewhere, and an era of boat-racing history was over.

But, if your urge is strong enough — he doesn't really want to sell them — call John Clark. He has nine 91 cubic-inch Van Blerck engines, and if he likes you he might be able to talk Ralph Glass into building an "A-Z" boat for you, and your riding mechanic.

BOMBITA

15

It doesn't take a big boat to make a big splash. It's more a matter of being in the right place at the right time... and the right speed. And making a splash doesn't always generate a lot of good will, even when you've won the big race. Especially if the recipient of the splash is the President of the United States, and you've soaked him to the skin. And if Harry Truman is the President, chances are pretty good he'll tell you exactly what he thinks of you.

In 1947 Philip Sharples and *Bombita*, a decidedly small Class A racing runabout, won the race, made the Presidential splash, and had the benefit of a few choice words from Harry Truman. Here's how Sharples remembers it:

"Martin Haurin, a dentist in Bensalem, Pennsylvania on the Delaware River just above Philadelphia, had followed boat racing for a few years so he decided to design and build a small racing boat. He picked Class A Inboard Runabout, as opposed to hydroplane with a step in the hull. He built *Bombita* in 1939 and named her *Gooch*, his wife's nickname. He installed a 100 cubic-inch Graymarine Racing Fireball engine, won most of the races he entered, and in 1941 or 1942 set a Class A world mile record, around 46 miles per hour.

"Racing stopped when the U.S. entered the war, and Haurin sold *Gooch* to Pete Ruth, who had a Class D racing runabout, named Bomba by his Spanish wife. Ruth changed the boat's name from *Gooch* to *Bombita*. Ruth sold *Bombita* to me

in early 1943 when he moved to South America.

"I was in the Navy, stationed at the Washington Naval Gun Factory doing aviation ordnance research work and awaiting completion

boat was twice as fast as mine, hydroplanes are notoriously bad in rough water and I decided I could beat him.

"We started together, two laps on a long oval course. I stayed behind him and let him go as slow as he wanted until the last turn. Turning a hydroplane in rough water is suicide.

"On the last turn, where he was at his worst, I zipped by him in my much better-handling runabout, and headed full throttle for the finish, about 300 yards away.

"I was out of the water more than in it. Although he tried, he couldn't catch me by the finish line.

"The yacht *Williamsburg*, with President Truman aboard on the fantail "porch," was at the finish line. The President saw how I had 'snookered' my opponent by staying behind him and then passing him in the last turn.

"At that point precisely the *Williamsburg* started off to take Truman back to port, leaving a big slick of flat water in its wake. I had to go in the same direction, so I headed down the slick, wide open, at her transom. At the last minute I turned to port to pass her, and was no longer protected.

"I hit one huge wave, went under the next wave, and came up soaked, going about three miles per hour. I looked to my right, and there, 20 feet away, was Truman and several others, with water from my splash pouring down them.

"Truman had his hat off, shaking it. He pointed at me with his other hand and yelled 'Nice work you son of a bitch, nice work you son of a bitch,' and then I was gone."

On September 27, 1947 in New Martinsville, West Virginia, Philip Sharples and *Bombita* set a new Class A mile straightaway world record: 47.629 miles per hour. Sharples subsequently

of an aircraft carrier on which I was to serve. I used *Bombita* only for recreation on the Potomac River.

"After the war in 1945 I started racing *Bombita* at various places on the Eastern Seaboard. We made major engine changes: to the carburetor, the intake and exhaust systems, the camshaft, the compression ratio. We increased the horsepower by about 10 percent. We won most of the races we were in (we ran out of gas once!) and

Bombita was the fastest boat in Class A.

"In September 1947 I won my class at the President's Cup Regatta in Washington. It was a rough day, and several race boats sank. At the end of the day there was a Free-For-All, any boat in any class. The trophy was a 26 inch sterling silver platter.

"It was so rough no one wanted to risk their boat. Finally, a 225 cubic-inch hydroplane — he wanted the trophy too — came out. Although his sold *Bombita's* Graymarine Racing Fireball engine and retired *Bombita* to his father's barn.

Bombita was resurrected in 1987 and Sharples, for the sake of convenience, re-powered her with a Volkswagen Rabbit engine. The new engine fits perfectly, and although it's similar in displacement to the "Fireball," *Bombita* runs at over 50 miles per hour now. Modern engines are just more efficient.

After the late 1940s, the A Inboard Runabout Class withered and died. But if you're interested, check that record book: Philip Sharples' and *Bombita's* mile run, 47.629 miles per hour, Class A Inboard Runabout, still stands.

World's Record.

MISS DAYTONA

16

According to her current owner, Philip Sharples, "*Miss Daytona* handles like a baby carriage at anything up to 30 miles per hour. "She banks inward and turns in very tight circles. Over 30 miles per hour she becomes a true flying machine. She'll scare the bejesus out of you if you don't know what you're doing.

"She's a 16 foot boat running a supercharged engine rated at 188 horsepower at 4,200 rpm that will turn over 5,000 rpm and produce 250 horsepower on 115 octane racing fuel.

She was probably designed by Cliff Hadley, and built in 1929 by Bruno Beckhard for Christopher Ripp. We don't know yet how fast she'll go," Sharples admits. "Probably somewhere in the 60s."

Originally raced by Al Louvett for Ripp, *Miss Daytona* was one boat in a stable that included two other exceptionally fast 151 Class hydroplanes, *Miss Meadowmeare* and *Bayhead*. *Miss Daytona's* engine, a supercharged 151 cubic-inch Miller Marine — by the legendary Harry Miller — represents a milestone in marine and automotive history.

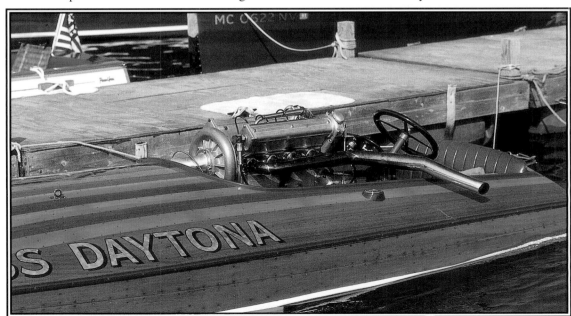

CAT'S PJS

She's a 1929 flat-deck Chris-Craft runabout. Flashy yet dignified. The Cat's Pajamas, a speedboat for Scott and Zelda in the last year of flapper fun. At 24 feet she's the smallest of two flat-deck models. Her larger sister ship came in at 26 feet. And she's the direct predecessor of the contemporary 24 foot Chris-Craft upswept runabout patterned after the 1930 model 103, now built brand-new by the Chris-Craft Motorboat Company for 1990s admirers of vintage mahogany craftsmanship.

Vince Bober purchased *Cat's PJs* in 1977 from Skip Gauger, who brought her up from Lake George. From 1977 to 1990 Bober ran the boat out of his Alton Bay boathouse on Lake Winnipesaukee. In 1990 *Cat's PJs* made the transcontinental trip to Lake Tahoe and to Bryte Johnson, who owns her now.

She's the same, but she's not the same. When Bober purchased the boat she had no name, and her hull sides were black.

"Remember," Bober reminds us, "Chris-Craft was a production boat. They had interchangeable parts. If you busted a plank, you could write Chris-Craft and they'd send you the plank you needed, cut to fit. And this was 1929, so not all the mahogany was perfect. When the best wood came in, it probably went into the shop foreman's boat, or his brother-in-law's. If the planks were mismatched, or the wood had small irregularities, Chris-Craft would paint the hull flat black and put varnish over it.

"We named her *Cat's PJs*, stripped the sides, and put on the Dietrich-style top. The wood looked awfully good. I believe she's at least 90 percent original. First I faired the hull, and then I got carried away and did everything. There may have been a plank replaced here and there, but she's mostly what she was when she came out of the factory.

"In those days there were two different tops, the Dietrich and the Crow. The Dietrich is a little fancier, a little more formal. We're not sure she originally had a top, and if she did it was probably the Crow, but my son, Vince Jr., and I manufacture Dietrich-style tops, so we put one on her."

George Johnson, also of Lake Winnipesaukee, and known as "The World's Largest Unauthorized Chris-Craft Dealer" because of his intimate knowledge of the history of the marque, suggests that the 24 foot flat deck was built from 1927 through 1929.

"They probably made about 500 of them, but don't quote me... The 26 footer was the most popular, with about 700 built. I've got it in my files somewhere here... The big one, the 28 footer, was always built in the upswept, or 'raised-deck' style. In 1930 they changed the 24 footer to imitate the raised-deck model, and that's the one they're building now."

In 1991, new boat buyers can purchase FRP (Fiberglass Reinforced Plastic), ferrocement, or concrete, if you're looking for a heavy boat; and aluminum, if you value practicality.

Ah yes, mahogany. The pendulum swings.

AURORA &
ALGOMA 18

Passions run deep. What is fact and what is opinion? The evidence is that *Aurora* and *Algoma* are in spirit, if not in fact, sisterships. Both of these 26 foot runabouts — similar in appearance — are currently acknowledged to be the hand-built products of the Bracebridge, Ontario craftsman Earl Barnes.

At the Toronto, Ontario, Winter Boat Show of 1983 Steve Lapkin, known to many as Staff Commodore and the more-than-able organizer of the Tahoe Yacht Club's Annual *Concour*s, identified Algoma as a Barnes runabout. But in a moment of reticence, Lapkin found himself unable to contradict the owner of the boat, John Aird.

"John Aird thought the boat was a Minett. He was the Lieutenant Governor of Canada — the Queen's appointee. It would be like me telling the president of the United States he's wrong and I'm right."

Perhaps, for the sake of international diplomacy, Steve Lapkin was reticent. And if John Aird was mistaken on the provenance of *Algoma*, it was a natural mistake.

She could easily be a Minett. Earl Barnes had served an apprenticeship under Bert Minett and undoubtedly Barnes' designs exhibit the influence of his mentor. More importantly, the quality of Barnes' workmanship lives up to Bert Minett's high standards. And most importantly, Barnes' boats were not at that time well known. He started building in 1927, and sources differ,

ALGOMA

but it is suggested that he may have built "Barnes" launches between 1927 and 1930 or that he may have continued until 1937. His total output is presumed to have been 20-30 boats, of which 14 have confirmed documentation.

B U N C O

C ome summer on Lake Winnipesaukee you can often find the Hopgood clan at their Tuftonboro camp, "Hoppiness," and down at the dock, riding peacefully over the small Winnipesaukee swells is *Bunco* – Dick Hopgood's pride and joy. *Bunco's* mahogany planks, like those of her 28 foot Gar Wood sisterships, quietly whisper the language of racing boat history, while her vintage six-cylinder, 225 horsepower Scripps engine speaks more loudly of speed and spray.

When *Bunco's* keel was laid down in 1930, Dick Hopgood's birth was 18 years into the future. As legend has it, these were tumultuous years for *Bunco*.

With Gar Wood hull #3000, *Bunco* — and it is presumed this is the boat's original name — was probably delivered to a home port somewhere on the Connecticut coast. The Gallup family, of Stone End Lodge on Lake Sunapee, New Hampshire, found *Bunco* high and dry, stored behind a marina somewhere around Bridgeport, Connecticut, if memory serves. In 1946 the Gallups re-powered *Bunco* with the current Scripps 208 engine, a later model of the 202 Scripps that probably powered her at christening. They had to.

According to the legend, *Bunco*, up to no good, was sunk off the Connecticut coast sometime in the early '30s, probably by the U.S. Coast Guard. The Coast Guard, sources say, refuses to confirm or deny.

FLIP - A - COIN 20

I t is a matter of both tradition and practicality that on the water, a boat can have only one Captain. More than one Captain is a scenario for mutiny, and the name of *Flip-A-Coin* is, if not the result of mutiny, the result of a disagreement between gentlemen.

A *concours* example of a 1930 27 foot, Ditchburn Viking Class runabout, *Flip-A-Coin* — "mother-in-law seat," stepped hull, vintage Sterling Petrel double-ignition engine and all — now belongs to Thomas I. "Toby" Hull of North Bohemia Island on Lake Rosseau.

Mr. Hull purchased the boat in 1973, in partnership with Canadian antique boat collector Tim Chisholm. According to the *Toronto Star* of August 20, 1979, "The partnership was unworkable, and they decided to end it... one of them would buy the other fellow out.

"Unfortunately, neither man was willing to give up his share. They settled the matter by tossing a coin..." *Betty Mac* became *Flip-A-Coin* and Toby Hull became her Master.

TRIPLE CHOICE 21

There are those who believe that life is a matter of control. In the restoration shop nothing could be more true. Antique valves are reground to the thousandths of an inch, electronic dash instruments are delicately wound, and may the gods have mercy on the innocent who would attempt to varnish a sanded mahogany hull in a workshop that is less than perfectly dust-free.

Life rewards those who sail into unknown bays, just to see the scenery. Those who would explore an unknown cove; those who venture into uncharted waters.

When Bill Munro found *Triple Choice* in 1987, he wasn't venturing into uncharted waters, but he wasn't looking for a 1930 26 foot Hacker triple-cockpit, either. Bill had something else in mind. But the tide was running in a different direction, and he discovered *Triple Choice*.

The Hacker's original owner, Mort Luffer, took delivery at Crooked Lake, Michigan, in 1930. As far as Bill Munro can tell, *Triple Choice* has never had a full restoration.

Old cars in *concours* condition rarely see the road. In the northern climes the season may be short, but for antique boat owners, summer and warm water beckon. Perhaps because *Triple Choice* has always been used, exploring coves and bays, her planks and timbers always in water, her hull has lasted over 60 years.

Munro stripped her down to bare wood for an immaculate varnish job. He replaced the upholstery. And back in the shop he rebuilt the 225 Kermath Seawolf engine, grinding all four valves for each of the six cylinders, rebuilding her twin carbs, and refurbishing her two distributors and twin ignition systems.

When he bought *Triple Choice*, Bill Munro was actually looking for a Chris-Craft Custom 27 foot runabout. And he later found her. *Sugar Lady* is her name, and she took "Antique Boat of the Year" at Clayton in 1992. But *Triple Choice*, not to be overshadowed, has remained an integral part of the Munro family for over five years. She may not now be a *concours* boat, but her Kermath engine is strong and her stout timbers on more than one occasion have ferried the four Munros across Lake Fenton for dinner at the Moose, and explored the waters of Munro's new home on Lake Charlevoix.

"In 1930," Munro attests, "Hacker was ahead of the competition. A Hacker was the Duesenberg of boats."

The job of moving fast over water hasn't changed much since then. Hull shape, propulsion, and the quality of craftsmanship are matters of control. Dignity, elegance, aesthetics: these are issues between men and gods. Sometimes, the Muse chooses to whisper in the artist's ear. If the artist has a sensibility, a feel for the curve of the mahogany, an eye for the crown of a deck, he might design a boat of lasting beauty.

In 1930 someone did. Triple-cockpit runabouts: 26, 28, 30, and a few 32 feet in length. John Hacker was his name, and *Triple Choice* was one of his creations.

RU SERIOUS 22

During the first decades of the 20th century, fast boats on water successfully seduced almost all those exposed to them. Men of wealth, education, and otherwise rational judgment were no more immune than the thousands who flocked to see Gold Cup races on the Detroit River, the St. Lawrence, and in Long Island Sound.

William Steinway, whose family heritage of fine craftsmanship in wood and metal made the Steinway name synonomous with excellence in pianos, entered briefly into the boatbuilding business prior to the turn of the century. Steinway was to discover, as did many others, that although it was inestimably difficult to produce beautiful boats, it was even harder to make money selling them.

After a financially disastrous contract to supply Eagle Submarine Hunters to the Navy during the Great War, Henry Ford reconsidered plans to produce with John L. Hacker a "Flivverboat."

Horace Elgin Dodge, Jr., may have been just another victim of an all-too-understandable enthusiasm. His father and uncle, the "Dodge Brothers," had manufactured parts for Henry Ford, and later amassed a fortune manufacturing the Dodge automobile.

At the 1923 New York Boat Show, Elgin Dodge announced a soon-to-be-unveiled line of boats called Dodge Watercars to be produced by the Horace E. Dodge Boat Works.

According to D.W. Fostle's *Speedboat*, Elgin Dodge had, by 1926 sunk almost $1 million into the Dodge Boat Works, whose activities included three George Crouch-designed boats entered in the 1925 Gold Cup. Almost two thirds of Dodge's million was irretrievably lost.

In 1924 Dodge Boat Works had hired George F. Crouch as designer and vice-president. Crouch, whose design portfolio included by then *Baby Bootlegger* and *Miss Columbia*, had a brief tenure with Dodge — just less than three years — but the influence of his inspired designs lasted longer than the job.

Built in 1931 by the Horace E. Dodge Boat and Plane Company — the new name that followed the 1930 dissolution of the Dodge Boat Works — *R U Serious*, Larry Ginsburg's 22 foot split-cockpit Dodge, illustrates the influence of the original George Crouch design.

The 22 foot Dodge had always been the company's most successful model. She was originally available powered by a 30 horsepower Dodge car engine, in keeping with Elgin Dodge's Watercar concept. A war-surplus 90 horsepower Curtiss V8, providing 35 miles per hour, was an option. *R U Serious* boasts a later stock 125 horsepower Lycoming V8, and top speeds in the same range as the war-surplus Curtiss.

One of about five or six of this model extant, *R U Serious* is notable for the exclusivity of her fittings. She has twin fold-down V windshields, an original (showroom stock) Duesenburg auto steering wheel, and hardware similar to that used on Gar Wood boats presumably by the same designer. Her bow light is integrated into the bow cleat. The sculpted mermaid bow ornament provides a final, elegant touch.

KATHRYN

For the tyros who come to the Annual Tahoe Yacht Club *Concours* to admire for the first time the fine old boats of yesterday, there are many examples of gifted design and craftsmanship. To Tahoe old-timers, the boats on display have a richer meaning, reaching back into childhood, the myth and the legend of Tahoe's past.

The *Concours* is a stunning display of boating history, although some of Tahoe's best boats just aren't there. But if tradition and history and spirit count, B.C. "Short" Wheeler's *Kathryn* is the queen of this Tahoe fleet.

First launched at Tahoe in 1931, *Kathryn* is not Tahoe's oldest boat. Though she's fast, she's not Tahoe's fastest boat. At 33 feet she's long, but not Tahoe's longest boat. And she won't win best of show at the *Concours* this year. Not all, but many of her 60 Tahoe summers can be seen in her varnished mahogany decks. She's a Gar Wood triple-cockpit runabout, and a boat with more than enough character to match the men whose legendary histories she helped make.

Kathryn was sold by Jacob P. "Jake" Obexer in 1931 to Arthur K. Bourne. Christened *Dispatch*, she was launched on a July Sunday at Obexer's about a mile north on the West Shore, presumably just in time to see the boat races (and appurtenant festivities) down at Chambers.

She was purchased from Bourne by Tahoe's Golden Boy, the charming, handsome, more-than-wealthy R. Stanley Dollar, Jr., who during the thirties made a habit of trading Tahoe's most prestigious racing trophies with Henry J. Kaiser. Dollar changed the boat's name to *Wychwood* and, (of course) replaced her original 425 horse-power Liberty V12 engine with a prototype marine conversion of a V12 Curtiss Conqueror aircraft engine, a larger power plant rated for 625 horsepower.

R. Stanley Dollar, Jr. and his father and family made a lot of local history. In Lake Tahoe the name Dollar evokes rich images of summer perfection. Dollar Point is named after them — it's a memory of real people. As owners of Sierra Boat, the Dollars gave Dick Clarke his job there.

It must have been Dollar's intuition and good judgment that put Dick Clarke at the helm of a business which perfectly matched his temperament, making him the jealous and protective curator of the more than 300 old boats he has defended with more than a parent's devotion.

Before the Dollars, more than anyone else, Jake Obexer was the progenitor of the Lake Tahoe speedboat tradition. When Obexer first viewed Tahoe in 1911, there's a good chance that the Lake may have looked much like Mark Twain's vintage 19th-century mother-lode description in *Roughing It*, despite turn-of-the-century logging operations.

By 1919 Obexer had relocated from Tahoe City to Homewood. He largely was Homewood.

There was Obexer General Merchandise, Gas and Oils, Obexer's Market (and U.S. Post Office), and Obexer's Garage. Jake Obexer brought exotic Gar Wood boats out from Michigan, and made Gar Wood forever the boat of choice at Lake Tahoe. He was a salesman, but he wasn't pushy — Tahoe's sophisticated clientele would have rebelled. Obexer sold by virtue of his contagious enthusiasm.

And as much as Gar Wood is Tahoe's boat, the lake's West Shore, and Homewood, is traditional Lake Tahoe. At Tahoe Yacht Club parties, Obexer's name always comes up. Although perhaps apocryphal, everyone's favorite story is about the time Jake was working down in the bilges on one of his client's boats. The boat was tied up in Obexer's boathouse. For some reason — probably an excess of enthusiasm — Jake forgot to vent the engine before crawling down into

the bilges for a little maintenance. The story always differs here, but many claim that Jake just had to light that cigar. It was spontaneous ignition, of course. The story always ends the same: Jake Obexer was blown through the roof and landed, safe but wiser, 60 feet out into Lake Tahoe. It's probably a lie.

The boathouse is gone, but Obexer's is still there in Homewood.

This is a little of the history that *Kathryn* represents to Lake Tahoe. And who better to carry on the Tahoe tradition than Short Wheeler, *Kathryn's* current owner?

Short — he isn't — bought the boat in 1971. For twenty years Wheelers have been navigating Tahoe in *Kathryn* looking for fun. Short replaced the original prototype Curtiss Conqueror with an updated, though vintage, production Curtiss. Short denies installing the siren on the bow: "It

was there when I bought her. It's pretty loud." Nonetheless, every now and then "in direct proportion to the amount of alcohol consumed," he'll give the siren a good blast, just to let people know *Kathryn* has arrived and the fun can begin.

And yes, they tell stories of Short Wheeler. Reliable sources say that, at 625 horsepower, the Curtiss engine probably has a little too much power for a 60 year-old hull. The boys are a little worried about Short. Who knows, there may be on Tahoe's cold and deep waters such a thing as going too fast.

These same sources — who would rather remain anonymous — suggest that for years Sierra Boat has been intentionally de-tuning the Curtiss engine, worried that, like Jake Obexer, Short, in an excess of enthusiasm, might have too much fun.

It's probably a lie.

W A M P U M 24

To some, Ted Valpey is known as a banker and a businessman, involved in the manufacturing of frequency-controlled radio crystals and in the early development of fiber optics. To others, he's best known as owner of Channel Marine in the Weirs on Lake Winnipesaukee. Yet, to many others, he and his wife Katy are known as the owners of *Jessica*, an elegant, almost 76 foot, 1930 Consolidated Commuter. And around the Owl's Head Transportation Museum in Rockland, Maine, Ted is known as an avid antique truck collector.

So, how does Ted Valpey of Dover, New Hampshire, see himself?

"I'm a junk collector. All I do is keep things.

We built a barn to put all the trucks in — I have about 25 — and I ask people if they want to see my junk collection."

Few would suggest that Ted Valpey's 1931 33 foot Gar Wood triple-cockpit runabout, *Wampum*, is junk. *Au contraire.*

Although she's rarely been shown, she's won Best of Show at the Lake Winnipesaukee ACBS gathering. She's been restored twice. Her current Curtiss model D12, a V12 aircraft engine, was built by Harold Rivard, the artist of engine builders.

Wampum's most recent restoration was done by Mark Mason of New England Boat and Motor, and did more than establish her thoroughbred credentials.

Kathryn, out on Lake Tahoe, is another 33 foot Gar Wood triple-cockpit runabout with the big Curtiss, "and I heard they found a third somewhere," says Valpey. So there just aren't that many of those big, beautiful and authentic Gar Woods left.

When Valpey, in partnership with his brother Bob, first purchased *Wampum* in the early 1970s, her provenance was clear. Then named *Sea Robin*, she had been stablemate to *Bunco* at Stone End Lodge on Lake Sunapee. *Sea Robin* was powered by a Scripps V12, but for the innovative Valpey brothers this wasn't quite enough. In a move that speaks more of lust for speed and danger than authenticity although by tradition racing runabouts have been powered by all manner of engine, the Valpeys installed an Allison aircraft engine. The same Allison that was known as the powerplant for some models of the formidable World War II P-51 Mustang and P-38 Lightning fighter aircraft.

This creative modification may or may not have been a mistake. "Bob found the Allison down in New York City. It was a brand new engine, still in the crate. With the supercharger it puts out about 1400 horsepower. This one without the supercharger puts out more than 900 horsepower.

"We had to build special hatches to accommodate the engine.

"When Mark Mason finally got her going, she was a little bow-heavy. It scared me so I decided to take the Allison out.

"I was afraid the torque would make the boat roll in the trough of a beam sea. This happened to a fellow in a 33 foot Baby Gar up on Lake Champlain."

Oh well, once again too much fun.

Which doesn't mean that Ted Valpey's love for unusual combinations has been dampened a bit. In 1988 he showed up at the Owl's Head Transportation Museum — Bob says it's really an antique aircraft museum — Vintage Truck Show at the wheel of his 1955 International Harvester "Emeryville" truck.

You can probably guess which triple cockpit Gar Wood Ted Valpey trailered behind it.

WEE GAR

25

For the most part, the appreciation of antique wooden speedboats is a new phenomenon. Until the early 1970s, vintage boats were as likely to find their way to the fireplace as the restorer's shop.

In search of something of value, a few individuals and society as a whole had the presence of mind to look to the past for the substance that seemed to be missing in contemporary America.

Society depends on the unobstructed vision of the young — and young at heart — to guide the way into the future, so it comes as no surprise that the appreciation of old boats is in no way limited to the old codgers for whom fast wooden boats remain a memory of youth.

Wee Gar is the embodiment of the vision of a young man, who, with the support of his father, brought new life to an old boat.

Aided by Chris Smith, Gar Wood's chronic success in powerboat racing created a demand for boats flying the Gar Wood burgee, and initially for the elite 33 foot runabout called a "Baby Gar."

The list of early "Baby Gar" owners included many of America's most successful wealthy sportsmen, names as well known in business as the "Baby Gar" was to become in power boating. In the face of growing demand, Wood decided to build a large plant in Marysville, Michigan, but when production began at the new factory in 1930, demand for Wood's custom-quality production boats was already on the wane, a victim

of the Great Depression. In 1932 the 18 foot split-cockpit Gar Wood runabout was introduced, a boat, by virtue of its size, of more modest price.

Bryan Turner's 1932 18 foot *Wee Gar* is one of only three 18 foot Gar Woods listed in the current Gar Wood Society directory.

Bryan, who grew up in Sacramento, inherited his love for old wooden speedboats. They

were an important part of his childhood summers. His great-grandmother had purchased waterfront property at Homewood on Lake Tahoe in 1906, despite the objections of her peers who were offended by the Indians who then bathed in the lake. After graduating from college, Bryan spent a year in Washington, D.C. working for the Republican National Committee, tracking candidates for the upcoming presidential elections. As a part of his job, he monitored every newspaper in the nation; but unlike his co-workers he spent most of his lunch hours and free time scouring the classifieds, looking at papers from upstate New York, New Hampshire, and the lake and river-rich areas of the Midwest. His perseverance paid off.

Before his return to California, Bryan discovered *Beth*, an almost perfect one-owner 18 footer that had spent the last 25 years tucked away in a barn on Lake Winola, Pennsylvania, sitting on her original 1932 Gar Wood shipping cradle.

Still, Emily Campbell, whose father had originally purchased the boat, was in no hurry to part with her. To view *Beth*, Bryan was forced to remove decades' worth of accumulated earth that prevented the opening of the barn doors. When Bryan bought the boat, and *Beth* was loaded on her trailer for the long trip to California, Lake Winola old-timers gathered in farewell — a sad goodbye to a Gar Wood that was a well loved part of local history and childhood memories.

But boats, like people, thrive on attention, and *Beth* was on her way to a good home. Bryan and his father, Howard Turner, who had helped with the original purchase, proceeded with an essentially in-house family restoration.

The engine, a Graymarine 118 horsepower six that replaced the 55 horsepower Chrysler with which *Beth* had been purchased, was absolutely authentic — Gar Wood had offered it as an option after the 18 footer's introduction. And the Gray was in good shape, having been "pickled," or stored with oil introduced into the cylinders, and the battery removed.

Interior planks, damaged by oil left in the bilges, were replaced. The layer of canvas that sealed the interior planking from the exterior planking was resined, and a few exterior planks below the waterline were replaced. All the bungs, the mahogany plugs that cover the hull fastenings, were popped, and every plank refastened. Woodwork beyond the scope of the Turners' ability was handled by Gary Minnis, a cousin, and Glory Beall, Lake Tahoe's antique wooden boat matriarch, supplied advice and emotional support.

Beth, re-christened *Wee Gar*, went into the water in August of 1988, the morning of the Tahoe Yacht Club's *Concours d'Elegance*. On the trip across the lake to the show, the engine hatch-covers were left open while Bryan prayed that the paint would be dry by the time he arrived at the Tahoe Boat Company marina. *Wee Gar* did well in the judging, but Bryan ascribes that to her rarity. No one had seen an 18 foot Gar Wood before.

Although Bryan exhibits her at the *Concours*, *Wee Gar* is not a "no-go show boat."

Every summer Bryan takes her out on a daily basis. She handles like the thoroughbred she is. Her deep stem cuts the swells, and Bryan claims he can cross Tahoe "at full speed and barely spill your cocktail."

She's the perfect boat for a young man — fast, beautiful, and unique. Bryan often cruises *Wee Gar* to Chambers, Tahoe's historic waterfront tavern at McKinney Bay. Four generations of Turners have summered at Tahoe; at Chambers almost everyone knows *Wee Gar* and Bryan. It's a mandatory Chambers Punch for Bryan, Bryan's friends, his parents, his parents' friends....

Once every year he'll make the 75 mile cruise around Tahoe's shoreline, or join the local Homewood clan on a weekend picnic excursion to Emerald Bay.

Wee Gar is undoubtedly fulfilled. She's just shy of her sixth decade, and still has all the energy and beauty of her youth. And she's doing just what she was conceived to do — make people happy.

PAINTED LADY

26

Spend enough time flashing around in old wooden boats looking for adventure and you're sure to find it. Even if all you want to do is go fast. After all, these boats were made for adventure. And to *Painted Lady,* adventure is no stranger.

On Saturday, March 20, 1937, at the Biscayne Bay Regatta, *Painted Lady* set a one-mile straightaway world record for Class E Racing Runabouts.

A decade later, with Langdon Laws (Caleb Bragg's nephew) at the wheel, *Painted Lady* tangled with early season skim ice on Lake Placid, tearing two planks just above the chine and forcing Laws to race back to port at high speed with the holed hull riding up above the waterline.

Not to mention engines... Howard Morrow, *Lady's* first owner, who purchased her new in 1936, and drove her in the Biscayne Bay record run, blew up the original Lycoming Racing 6 engine in 1937. She was known then as *Miss Florida.*

Langdon Laws purchased the boat from Morrow in 1938, and Laws blew up the Lycoming in 1939, and again in 1947. This isn't a matter of placing blame.

On the water in a boat like *Painted Lady*, there's no such thing as too fast. It's more like skating on the edge of the abyss... if the hull can take it, and the pilot can take it, there's a constant and necessary temptation to push just a little harder. The problem and pleasure is that one never really knows how far one can go... sometimes

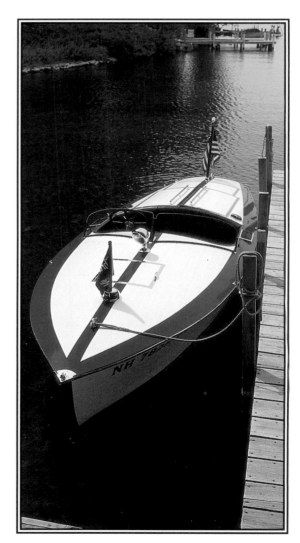

Mason did throw in an ultra-pneumo-built 350 Chevy, but he has owned and restored the most authentic antique boats in the nation, and he's allowed at least one go-fast boat with modern iron he can count on.

Maybe.

The crew is up early once again — nobody likes 5:30 wakeup calls, even for the sake of good photographs — and the indomitable Polly Pratt Brown is at the helm of *Painted Lady*.

There's no question of Polly's credentials. She's a Marblehead girl with a life-long boating history. She shoots and writes for *WoodenBoat*, and she knows the stem from the stern and the keel from the chine.

Mark's piloting the photo boat, and things look good. The sun is just beginning to show above the Winnipesaukee clouds. Polly's running *Painted Lady* almost full out, and Mark is excited. Every time Polly jumps a swell he cries out, "Did you get that, did you get that?" The motor drive is burning film.

Then there's a moment of hesitation. *Painted Lady's* riding low in the stern.

"She's sinking," Mark Mason yells.

It's Coast Guard regulation "Mayday" drill, all hands to the lines, get a line off her bow, quick, into shallow water, save the boat.

Nobody's happy. Nothing's quite as embarrassing as pushing an old boat too hard. Polly's wet, *Painted Lady* has a couple of inches of water washing her decks in the shallows, and there are three red faces on Lake Winnipesaukee.

But no harm's done. In two days *Painted Lady's* hull is patched — apparently she hit a rock in the shallow — and the historic boat has yet another adventure in her log book.

We've seen the abyss, and returned to talk about it. Again.

the center just doesn't hold. And the bottom of the abyss is a long way down.

Anyway, Laws — presumably tired of major overhauls — replaced the temperamental Lycoming in '47 with a Chrysler Crown. Perhaps he'd had too clear a view of the abyss. Whatever the reason, the boat went into storage at Dusseau's Marine at Lake Placid in 1947 and

didn't emerge until 1986, when she was purchased by Mark Mason.

Painted Lady hasn't changed much. Sure, she's got a new name, and Mark Mason replaced the two pine planks where Langdon Laws ran into skim ice. But she still has her original paint job, blue and white, American racing colors. The decks have never been stripped to bare wood.

WOODMERE 27

For some reason unknown, the things of the past often bring us the greatest pleasure: an old scarred hat, a hopeless pair of jeans, comfortable loafers well worn and many times resoled. These insubstantial but familiar items seem somehow to bring a sense of peace and security into our lives.

For most of us, a lakeside summer cottage in the woods remains only a pastoral dream. For a very few, it is reality. Some descendants of families blessed with stability and foresight still enjoy the same tranquil evenings and quiet shoreline nights beneath the same stars their grandparents enjoyed.

The human heart aches for those things lost: family, friends, youth, the courage of innocence, a sense of timelessness. These are things that cannot be bought.

Some will say it's superstition. But the wisdom of the ages tells us a boat has a soul.

Prove this gift of generations wrong.

Woodmere is a gift of generations. A prized inheritance that spans the years and vicissitudes of life.

She's well traveled. She's lived at Woodmere Island on Lake Rosseau in the Muskokas, and she's partied beneath the California sun on Lake Tahoe. She's a little bit eccentric — okay, she's the only Minett-Shields with a 1937 Cadillac dashboard — and she's a flirt. Her owner, Dan Hauserman, suggests that her port and starboard running lights, inset into the hull, create a mysterious peek-a-boo eyebrow effect as she cruises toward you. "If the flirtatious *Woodmere* could only tell her secrets, we'd know how many passengers she has pleased both day and night."

Dan Hauserman is the son of Earl and Mary Hauserman, of Cleveland Heights, Ohio, who bought Sagamore Island on Lake Rosseau in

MISS CATALINA V 28

In names there is romance. The syllables, the rhythm of the words, the memories. Like a scent from a long-ago experience in Proust's *A Remembrance of Things Past*, place names touch the imagination and the heart. Images — picture postcards — fill the mind, emotions are set free.

Santa Catalina Island and Avalon, Catalina's seaside village *touristique*, conjure the image of a carefree life, escape from worries, vacation fun. Big bands in the ballroom at the Avalon Casino. The earthy and elitist Tuna Club. Zane Grey, alone in a skiff, rowing out to horse a 200 pound yellowfin tuna from the channel. Yachts and speedboats, seaplanes and movie stars.

Southern California is an artificial oasis created by theft. It's a sordid history of developers and greed and a vast aqueduct to steal the fertility of the Owens Valley. Yet for 36 years, the Catalina Speedboat Company brought the thrill of speed on water to earth-bound Southern Californians. Between 1922 and 1958 a succession of six Catalina-built Bombard speedboats, Liberty-powered, gave the gift of spray and screams and offshore island views to Catalina visitors.

Miss Catalina V is a photograph of pre-war island play. The fifth boat in the series, as her name would imply, *Miss Catalina V* is 29 feet, 11 inches of oak and mahogany ribs, one-inch cedar planking, and glassy mahogany deck. She was launched in 1938 with, like her sisters, a mighty Liberty V12. Her odd length was no accident;

Coast Guard regulations required all passenger-carrying vessels thirty feet and over to be inspected and certified, so Al Bombard, her builder, and the Catalina Speedboat Company settled for one inch short, and no less fun.

When it was designed and built during the

First World War, the twelve-cylinder Liberty Aircraft engine was ahead of its time; but by 1938, when *Miss Catalina V* was launched, these venerable power plants had proven a little shaky. Legend suggests that Al Bombard, who served his apprenticeship with Liberty Motors Experimental Service, was concerned as much with practical reliability as romance, and kept three Liberty engines in reserve, overhauled and ready to go, for every engine currently in service.

The Liberty in *Miss Catalina V* holds 10 gallons of oil, burns approximately half a gallon of oil an hour, and blazes through 30 gallons of gasoline an hour. Almost everyone produced a marine conversion of the Liberty, with final power ratings from around 400 horsepower to over 500, but this particular model, a Capitol Marine Conversion Model LA-12, provides about 380 horsepower to the shaft. At sea level, off Catalina Island, the engine would speed *Miss Catalina V* to 55 miles per hour at 1725 revolutions per minute.

For Jim Koch, *Miss Catalina V's* owner, she's been a long time coming. The Sierra Boat restoration began in 1982. Eight years later *Miss Catalina V* bowed for her second debut at the 1990 Tahoe Yacht Club *Concours d'Elegance*. *Catalina V's* sistership, *Miss Catalina VI*, shares the waters of Lake Tahoe, but *Miss Catalina V* wins the laurel wreath. Her original power, as accurate a restoration as is possible, and her original configuration, win her Catalina honors.

This, then, is forever the mystery of steel and wood. An old boat, a funky engine. Sierra Boat, marine Mecca on a fabled lake. But how does one account for the enthusiasm of the many visitors who viewed *Miss Catalina V* during the eight years of her restoration? And how does one explain the re-lived moments of a youth lost, times gone by, days of fun and nights of romance at Santa Catalina Island?

Call it old boat magic!

MARY BRYTE

"I'll bet a case of whiskey that no one else out there has a 1938 stock twin-engine 22 foot Chris-Craft. Twin-engine Chris-Crafts are so rare that one *concours* judge told me I'd done a perfect job of converting the boat to twin engines. I just walked away."

Mary Bryte's owner, Jerry Johnson, is an old-time Tahoe character, so none of the locals will be surprised at his offer to wager. And stock twin-engine Chris-Crafts are extremely rare; a couple of others from this era have been documented, but Johnson claims "As far as we know, this is the only 22 footer with twin engines."

Scarcity notwithstanding, an inboard twin-engine layout has significant advantages in addition to speed. *Mary Bryte's* six-cylinder 131 horsepower Chris-Craft Hercules engines, one the standard KBL, the other KBO — O for opposite rotation — turn in different directions, negating the effect of the rotational torque of the propellers. The props turn to the outside, so the port side engine turns to the left and the starboard engine turns to the right. When docking, or more importantly, backing down, the boat drives straight and true.

In tight situations an accomplished pilot can play twin throttles and transmissions in symphony or syncopation. A twin-engine boat can work like a caterpillar tractor, one propeller in reverse and the other in forward, and turn around in its own length. Or the boat may be "walked," literally driven sideways, into a dock.

Which is not to say that twin engines with dual controls aren't an asset at speed. "That's how Gar Wood won the Harmsworth Trophy in

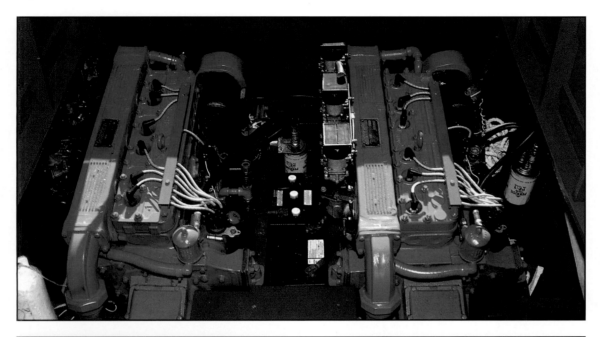

Miss America," Jerry Johnson contends. "When he rounded the buoys Wood throttled back on the inside engine and kept the throttle pegged on the outside engine. The drag from the slower-moving inside prop helped him turn tighter and get ahead in the curves."

Mary Bryte isn't exactly Miss America, but "you can call her a racing runabout," Jerry says. She tops out at about 50 miles per hour at sea level, a little slower at Tahoe's mile-high altitude. And she gulps gas, burning 17 gallons an hour "when I'm romping."

Small consideration though, in comparison to the cost of owning, restoring and maintaining a fifty-year-old wooden boat.

Jerry found Mary Bryte in Rocklin, California, in 1970. Because he had been a friend of Bruce Kennedy, who ordered the boat from the Tahoe Boat Company in 1938, he recognized her immediately. Kennedy, a Los Gatos, California, entrepreneur, had originally christened the boat Carolyn. Jerry Johnson renamed her Mary Bryte after his mother.

"The serial number #22125 was on the hull planks and on the backs of the seats in the second cockpit. They used to burn them in with a branding iron. I wrote Chris-Craft and they sent me copies of the original manifest, and photographs of her while she was being built. Because she had twin engines, Chris-Craft was constantly taking her off the assembly line, and they photographed her at various stages of her construction.

"I keep her at Obexer's year 'round; it's cool at Tahoe in the summer, so the planks don't shrink. Down in Sacramento, where I live, it's 110 degrees in the summer — not good for the planking. Tahoe is great for mahogany.

"After I bought her, Earl's Marine in Sacramento did the restoration. The compression

was okay, so even though we removed the engines we didn't do a low-end overhaul. We rebuilt the carburetors, removed the fittings, and took her down to bare wood. The boat was naked.

"We re-chromed the fittings, replaced the wiring that was down in the bilges and the hold — I've still got a bunch of original wiring up under the dashboard — and stained and varnished the hull. All the planks are original, although for the *concours* there are probably a couple that should be replaced.

"The dash is unusual; there are ten instruments. I figure Chris-Craft wanted to make it symmetrical, so they threw in an eight-day jeweled clock, wound by a ball and string. You see them on some of the big old Gar Woods. Ted Grebitus rebuilt the clock for me."

Jerry's a character but he's a man of his word, and his family's been at Tahoe since 1930. So if you own a 1938 22 foot twin-engine Chris-Craft, he'll make good on his offer. You can find him at Homewood.

And he's flexible: "If you don't like whiskey, I'll make it gin."

Sometimes in life decisions are made for all the wrong reasons. If boat purchases, and especially antique boat purchases, were always based on non-emotional, practical analysis, it's a pretty good guess that most of the boats featured in this book would still be in old barns, or (if they're lucky) in museums. Fortunately, many otherwise practical people have held their rational minds in momentary abeyance and bowed to passion. One can only guess how many times, with a sinking feeling in his stomach — the voice of practicality overruled — Man has said "It's beautiful, I like it, I want it, I'll take it."

In 1986, Bill Munro found *Chickie IV* at Snow Lake, Indiana, where she had been stored since 1955. He knew nothing about her, and perhaps his decision followed a similar thought process. There is little question that the satisfaction Bill has received from restoring, piloting and owning *Chickie IV* far outweighs any doubts he had when he bought her. At 15' 6" she's as small as a slipper, one of those boats that the pilot seems to wear more than drive, but in her racing colors, powered by her infamous Gray Racing Fireball engine, she looks and performs better than the law should allow.

Of course, she's been thrashed. She was built to be thrashed. History alleges that she was a gift to her original owner, Milford Buelow, from his father in 1939. A young man at the time, Buelow, whose Chicago family summered at Fox Lake, Illinois, wasted no time in embarrassing

other owners by his dominance of the local racing scene. When he was once beaten by a Fireball-powered boat in 1940, Milford Buelow ordered his own Gray Racing Fireball to replace *Chickie's*

original four-cylinder 81 horsepower Gray Phantom 4-75 engine.

With the addition of the new engine, and the deletion of her hull step, *Chickie IV* continued to race in the E Runabout Class through the early fifties — presumably restored to her position of dominance. By 1955 she was no longer competitive. Buelow removed the Racing Fireball and briefly installed it in a modern hydroplane. From 1955 to 1986, when Munro purchased her, *Chickie IV* remained in storage at Snow Lake, Indiana.

Ignorant of the boat's history, Munro set out on the paper chase so characteristic of antique-boat restoration. He was to be well rewarded.

An advertisement for old boating magazines resulted in the purchase of a couple of boxes of aging periodicals, and while thumbing through them Munro spotted a photo of *Chickie IV* in the December 1947 issue of *Lakeland Yachting*. In another serendipitous turn of fate, Munro called Skip Kramer at Fox Lake, Illinois.

As Munro described the boat to Kramer over the phone, there was an ominous silence at the other end of the line. Finally, Kramer spoke: "That's *Chickie* — I took the step out of the bottom." Kramer had vintage photos of *Chickie IV*, and subsequently introduced Munro to the original owner, Milt Buelow.

Because *Chickie IV* is a race boat, Munro decided to restore her to race condition, not stock. The hull step was replaced, and her varnished sides were gold-leafed with the proud Racing Fireball warpaint to match the vintage photos. Stock delivery of the Century Thunderbolt was with a black hull, so *Chickie IV*, custom-ordered with varnished sides, may be the only authentic varnished-hull Thunderbolt extant.

For Munro, with the mechanical background

of a Michigan native, working on the Fireball engine was a pleasure. The Fireball's carburetors, in the exotic "tarantula" three-barrel cluster, were part of the custom-built, racing-mill package that included aluminum intake and oil pans, a special racing cam, with forged

magnafluxed rods and a lightweight flywheel.

Munro completed a major overhaul, boring the cylinders and replacing the pistons. Doug Morin of Morin Mahogany Marine in Bay City, Michigan, did the woodwork, including the tough job of replacing the hull step.

Chickie IV's on Lake Fenton now, with *The Fifth* and *Triple Choice* and the rest of Bill Munro's small fleet of antiques, but he still trailers *Chickie IV* around to a few shows to exhibit. She may be old, but in her Fireball racing colors she's still mean and dangerous and fast.

THE BARRELBACKS 31

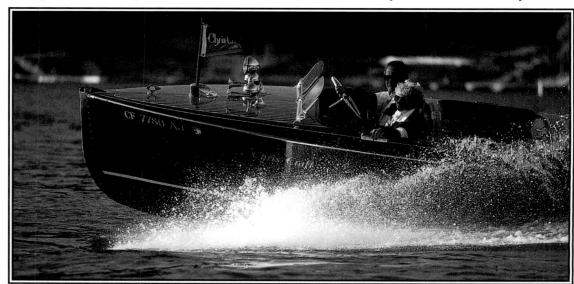

LICKETY SPLIT

Old boats have a kind of historical authenticity, a discrete sequence of events and locations, a finite placement in time that parallels the lives of their designers, manufacturers, owners and their friends, and even the wider scope of world events.

Beyond these specifics, boats establish or inherit a value, an abstract importance above their physical presence. They become more than a mere amalgam of steel and wood.

Some old boats, the important ones, are surviving emblems of the spirit of an age, the physical representation of an outlook on life: like the Brancusi sculpture "Flight," the embodiment of a concept.

Beginning in 1937 with the first offering of the 16 footer, Chris-Craft designed, built and marketed the series of boats that was to become the very image of the mahogany speedboat: the Chris-Craft "barrelback" runabout.

In 1937 America and Chris-Craft were emerging from the depths of both emotional and financial depression. The new boats signified a change in attitude. While pleasure was not something to be expected from life, it was certainly allowed.

Erroneously referred to at times by some as

MISS ARROWHEAD

"torpedo-sterns," the barrelback runabouts were built between 1937 and 1941, when the design and production capabilities of Chris-Craft were directed away from the pursuit of pleasure toward the national effort to win the war. A few pleasure boats, those on the production line in 1941 and not marketed until 1942, represent the end of the barrelback era. The end of a brief period in time between depression and war.

The barrelbacks were offered in a panoply of sizes, from the 16 footer to 17, 19, 22 and 23 footers, and even through the extremely rare 27 foot runabout.

Whether at home on Lake George, on Lake Tahoe, on Southern California's Lake Arrowhead or on Europe's Cote d'Azur, the Chris-Craft barrelback runabout was and remains America's image of *the* flashy pre-war speedboat.

Lickety Split is a California Chris-Craft, a 1940 23 foot, triple-cockpit runabout. New, she was delivered to San Francisco with a 6 cylinder Chris-Craft Hercules engine. Now a transplant to Larry Ginsberg's Southern California fleet, she spent most of her life on Clear Lake in California's San Joaquin "Big" Valley. Her twin "Bugatti" windshields mark the historic turning point from the flat Chris-Craft windshields of the

1930s to the elite and briefly produced "V" windshields of the 1940s.

Built in 1941, *Miss Arrowhead* was brought by Dick Clarke from Southern California, restored, and now makes her home under the boathouse of Scott Hedrick in Dollar Point, Lake Tahoe. Hedrick, himself a transplant from Southern California, says, "I know my sons will grow up, get married, and have careers of their own. But I'll always keep *Miss Arrowhead* and our Tahoe summer home, and let the boys know they're welcome to come up for a week in the summer and use the boat. They'll be here."

When *The Fifth*, a single-step Chris-Craft "Racing Hydroplane," was delivered in 1941 she was accompanied by a warning, like contemporary warnings on alcohol and tobacco, that she

was "For Racing Only." Chris-Craft apparently knew that this 16 footer would be a temptation to hubris, more fun than the gods would practically or logically allow.

Unlike most hard-chine boats, the racing hydroplane slides around the curves instead of banking into them. Chris-Craft must have expected that at least a few neophyte drivers would flip, and probably more than a few of them did. Chris-Craft delivered the boat with a high-performance 121 horsepower KB engine with three in-line carburetors that protruded above the low deckline. The streamlined red fairing, designed to shield the carburetors, came to symbolize one of the fastest and most desirable Chris-Craft boats of the pre-war years.

The Fifth is currently owned by Bill Munro of Lake Fenton, Michigan.

THE FIFTH

ACKNOWLEDGMENTS

To say that this book is my own would be nonsense. If there is any single explanation for this book's existence, it is the fact that antique boats generate love and enthusiasm. People I had never met were willing to share their time, to provide emotional, logistical and historical support, to invite me into their lives and family histories.

My greatest pleasure in the pursuit of this project has been the intimacy I've established and the time on the water I've shared with others who are passionate about boats.

If the word obsession is used in this book, it should be understood that an obsession is only an ultimately strong form of passion without which our lives are like those described by Thoreau: "Lives of quiet desperation."

It is my hope that you will bear with me. The list is long. Many who have made this book possible are important mainly to me; many are the men and women whose dedication, foresight and commitment rescued and restored the important speedboats and launches of history. My father, George Perry Duncan, has provided the kind of support — both emotional and practical — that is motivated only by faith.

I will forever regret that none of the Clark family boats are included in this book. Since 1883, generations of Clarks have summered at Comfort Island on the St. Lawrence River near Alexandria Bay. It was there in 1973 that I first fell in love with old wooden boats. *Buzz*, a 1910 launch, remains suspended from the Comfort boathouse ceiling. To Tad and Kira Clark, Deborah Clark, good old Mansel, I hope "Thanks" will be enough.

It is my great pride to be included in one of the two volumes of

Comfort Island guest books that document well over a hundred years of hospitality and fun.

Only those who know him can have an inkling of Mark Mason's obsession with old boats. As much detective as restorer, he's spent countless hours in libraries, going through old boat magazines, searching for the clues that illuminate our knowledge of the best of the past. If anybody knows boat history, especially racing-boat history, Mark Mason does. I hope that this book comes up to his high standards.

And thanks to Polly Brown, whose spirit and enthusiasm fired up the early morning shoots.

Thanks to always-busy Dick Clarke of Sierra Boat Company, Carnelian Bay, Lake Tahoe. Thanks for being who you are and doing what you have done.

Lake Tahoe is the hardest place to photograph boats. Not because the Sierra light isn't perfect, and not because the boats aren't there, but because there are just too many distractions. Chambers Landing always beckons — some of the old boats just steer themselves to Chambers for a cocktail — and the food at Sunnyside is great. Or you might, if you're lucky, hang around "Playtime," the Turners' long-time family cabin at Homewood, and drink and laugh with Commodore Happy Howard and Kay and their son Bryan. Thanks, Bryan. And the whole Homewood Snoop Patrol.

Wimur Lodge, the Woodruff family cottage on Lake Joseph in the Muskokas, is generations (1926) old. The gods were smiling. James and his parents extended their hospitality to a journalist from California that they had never met. Alone at night, I'm sure I heard the ghosts of Wimur walk the halls. The Woodruffs, Peter, their son-in-law, the dinner conversation...

and the boats. Thanks to James and everyone.

Dr. and Mrs. Charles Berletti deserve more than mention, and they know why! Likewise Dr. and Mrs. Eric Naumburg.

Mr. and Mrs. Bill Munro of Lake Fenton got me off after an early morning Michigan photo session in time to make my Detroit plane. Thanks for everything, and dinner at the Moose.

Scott and Corinne Hedrick of Lake Tahoe and Ross, California, put up with my early mornings and late nights and the day I stole their Cobalt for a photo boat. They're family, sort of, but that doesn't mean I'm forgiven. I hope time heals all wounds.

The inimitable Philip Sharples for the Thousand Islands and Tubac, Arizona, is an inspiration. He's in his seventies, and a little embarrassing, because no one will ever have as much energy and fun as Philip does.

Don Price of St. Lawrence Restoration, an old and true friend, John Clark especially, and Tom Frauenheim, and to the "Speedboys" everywhere, whether in name or spirit, thanks. Peter Hazzard, my old roommate from prep school — Millbrook — helped me through Boston on a jet-lag night and put me up at his Annisquam summer home on Cape Ann in Massachusetts. I'd gotten into trouble there when we were chasing girls in our youth. The Hazzards either forgot or forgave. Amen.

Dick and Patty Hopgood. We spent a righteous afternoon — Patty's birthday — cruising and playing in *Bunco* on Lake Winnipesaukee. I introduced them to the Tahoe concept of the "TD" speed cruise. Total Dignity. Fast enough to have fun, but not to spill your cocktail.

Scott at the Brooks Photo Center in Santa Barbara helped more than he knows. Ken Chadwick flew me up to Tahoe for a quick weekend of more fun than work. Steve Cook, Ph.D., was more than critical of my grammar.

Thanks to everyone who put up with my "Captain Bligh" antics when they were generous enough to drive the photo boat.

And it goes without saying, thanks to all the boat owners who gave up a morning's sleep or an evening's cocktail hour. You know who you are. Thanks for sharing.

Primarily, this is an oral history. Memories from youth, recollections of times past. Personal views through the mist of history. Anyone who has ever had the privilege of writing is more than aware that concrete and definitive history is a concept for the sophomoric. Writers write what they read, what they are told, what they experience, what they see.

Hopefully, the photographs are pleasing. Boat histories may be sketchy. This is not a scholarly work. Few things in life are more elusive than "Truth." Regrettably, one must presume that mistakes — errors of fact — have been made. They are all my own.

There are few readily available histories of antique power boats. None is more informative, better written, or more appropriately illustrated than D.W. Fostle's *Speedboat*. The Rodengens' *The Legend of Chris-Craft* is notable for its documentation of the early boating characters and their stormy relationships: Chris Smith, Baldy Ryan, Gar Wood. *prewar wood,* by Carol Van Etten, recounts the high life and fine times of the Lake Tahoe boating scene. *The Boatbuilders of Muskoka*, by A.H. Duke and W.M. Gray, portrays the lives and boats of what many believe to be the birthplace of the most perfect speedboats and launches in North America.

Every summer, fellow travelers Norm and Jim Wangard of *Classic Boating* battle inclement weather, unpredictable airline schedules and editorial deadlines — journalists in the trenches — to bring antique and classic boating news to enthusiasts. The Wangards were familiar faces and, unlike many journalists, non-competitive. Thanks and best wishes.

Finally, great thanks to Tom Toldrian, my publisher. As a mentor he has done his best to temper my idealism in the fire of practicality. Thanks, Tom for your patience and understanding and long-term support.

If it should appear that, overall, the project was too much fun, one makes no apologies. For if this book has any single unifying purpose it is to share the pleasures of time spent on the water in old wooden boats. To share with the reader what has been so generously shared with me. To communicate a little of the magic of old boats.

Robert Bruce Duncan
Santa Barbara, California

Book Design: Marge Michelman
Typography: Ginny Greenfield
Editor: David E. Gardella
Technical Editor: Joe Gribbins